Redundancy and renewal
Maintaining and using historic churches

Selected papers from the
Norwich Historic Churches Trust
conferences
2014 and 2015

Edited by Nicholas Groves

Lasse Press

Text © the contributors
Design © Curran Publishing Services Ltd

All rights reserved. No reproduction, copy or transmission of this
publication may be made without written permission.

No portion of this publication may be reproduced, copied or transmitted
save with written permission or in accordance with the provisions of the
Copyright, Designs and Patents Act 1988, or under the terms of any licence
permitting limited copying issued by the Copyright Licensing Agency,
Saffron House, 6–10 Kirby Street, London EC1N 8TS.

Any person who does any unauthorized act in relation to this publication may be liable
to criminal prosecution and civil claims for damages.

The authors have asserted their right to be identified as the author of this work in
accordance with the Copyright, Designs and Patents Act 1988.

First published 2016
by the Lasse Press
2 St Giles Terrace, Norwich NR2 1NS, UK
www.lassepress.com
lassepress@gmail.com

ISBN-13: 978-0-9933069-3-8

Typeset in Garamond and Stone Sans by
Curran Publishing Services Ltd, Norwich, UK

Printed in the UK by Imprint Digital, Exeter.

Front cover illustrations, clockwise from top left: Restoration of the ruined church of St Margaret, Hopton on Sea, Suffolk (photo Susan Curran); Sianagh Gallagher at the British Paraclimbing championships 2015 in St Benedict's Manchester (photo Natasha Hirst, courtesy of Womenclimb); a former almshouse bedroom now preserved as a museum at the Great Hospital, Norwich (photo Susan Curran); repair works (2016) at St Peter Hungate, Norwich (photo Susan Curran); maintenance survey training at St James, Freiston (© SPAB); All Saints, Bolton after regeneration (photo Churches Conservation Trust); sign for an exhibition at Holy Trinity, York (photo Steven Saxby); a former church for sale in Liverpool (photo Steven Saxby).

Contents

Foreword *Nick Williams*	v
Preface and acknowledgements *Nicholas Groves*	vii
Historic churches: heritage and voluntary action *Robert Piggott*	1
The use, reuse and abuse of 'alternative use': a historical perspective on the reappropriation of urban closed churches for other purposes *Steven Saxby*	19
Working co-operatively with closed churches: the Holland Coastal Group *Stella Jackson*	41
'With concern, but not without hope': an overview of the Norwich Historic Churches Trust *Nicholas Groves*	48
The Norwich Historic Churches Trust, returning churches to the community *Rory Quinn*	61
Heavenly Gardens *George Ishmael*	80
Confessions of a former tenant *Susan Curran*	86
Inspired by the past – engaging the present – securing the future. New uses for religious heritage at the Churches Conservation Trust *Peter Aiers, Matthew McKeague and Edward Walkington*	97
Index	*119*

Foreword

Nick Williams

This is the second volume of papers presented at conferences held by the Norwich Historic Churches Trust in 2014 and 2015. The first volume, *Of Churches, Toothache and Sheep*, was published earlier this year by the Lasse Press. Organized by Nicholas Groves and facilitated by the Trust, the conference papers covered a wide range of topics relating to the medieval church and alternative uses of church buildings.

That first volume focused largely on episodes and people related to the medieval church in Norfolk and farther afield. This volume addresses the many issues affecting how historic churches – many no longer used for worship – are preserved, maintained and made use of.

Robert Piggot's paper examines how historic places of worship in Norwich have been preserved, often at the initiative of volunteers, and how this process has increased public awareness of the need to preserve such a vital part of our heritage, and also influenced planning policy related to redundant churches and the wider cityscape.

The second paper, by Steven Saxby, casts its net wider, considering the varied approaches taken throughout England in finding alternative uses for former churches in urban areas. It includes examples of some of the more unusual uses, such as a climbing centre in Warrington.

In a brief report Stella Jackson provides an insight into community involvement in preserving a much-loved church. This was by means of a Maintenance Co-operative which took on the preservation of All Saints, Benington, Lincolnshire, working with the community to retain and protect it, and prevent it going the same way as other facilities in the village.

Four papers in this volume do not draw on conference presentations, but were written specifically for this book. First, Nicholas Groves, the editor of both volumes and the initiator of the conferences, provides an overview of the Norwich Historic Churches Trust – a body of which he is a long-serving trustee. The Trust was formed in 1973 to care for 18 of the city's medieval churches and to find suitable uses for them. Nicholas is well placed to provide such an overview with his extensive knowledge of the churches and their former use as places of worship.

Dovetailing neatly with the previous paper is one by Rory Quinn on the history of the Norwich Historic Churches Trust. Despite the constant battle to obtain funding, Rory recounts a story of accomplishment in the face of adversity, one in which he played a major role as the chair of the Trust for a decade.

George Ishmael is a landscape gardener who became an NHCT trustee, and provides an overview of his Heavenly Gardens initiative to improve the appearance and use of the churchyards to Norwich's medieval churches.

The final paper focusing specifically on the NHCT is from someone who has experienced two sides of the use and care of a redundant church. Susan Curran is a long-serving NHCT trustee and for a time was a tenant at St Mary Coslany, one of the churches in its care. She recalls with some nostalgia the travails of operating a business in a medieval building, not least of which was coping with winter temperatures in a building that was almost impossible to heat adequately.

Perhaps fittingly, the final paper, compiled by Edward Walkington and drawing on presentations by his colleagues Matthew McKeague (in 2014) and Peter Aiers (in 2015), explains the role of the Churches Conservation Trust which 'cares for the third largest historic estate in charitable ownership in the United Kingdom'. By the use of a series of case studies Edward provides a most stimulating endpiece.

This is a valuable contribution to the Trust's efforts to raise awareness of the issues surrounding the conservation and use of our heritage of medieval churches, both in Norwich and across the country. All profits from the volume will go to the NHCT to support its work.

Nick Williams is a former leader of Norwich City Council, and is currently chair of the Norwich Historic Churches Trust.

Preface and acknowledgements

This volume completes the publication of papers presented at the first two Conferences of the Norwich Historic Churches Trust. It was decided that, rather than publish the papers of each of the first two conferences as separate volumes, it made more sense to combine them, and publish thematically. So this volume takes reuse of churches as its theme, something which NHCT takes very seriously. Despite the wide variety of uses to which former churches are put, both in Norwich and elsewhere, their original purpose cannot be disregarded, and these uses must not be anything which would, as the manuals of Canon Law used to say, 'cause grave scandal'. In addition, parish churches (and medieval ones in particular) act as a focus for their community and its history, and this must be taken account of, also.

The volume falls into two sections: three papers dealing with the question of redundancy and reuse on a national scale, and four specially written for this volume, dealing with the NHCT, its genesis and history, the Heavenly Gardens project for the churchyards, and a view from a former tenant. It is rounded off with a contribution from our 'big sister', the Churches Conservation Trust, which is a national body, and has three of the Norwich churches in its care.

As before, my thanks go first to Stella Eglinton, the Trust's administrator, who assisted me with setting up the conferences, and the staff of the House of Prayer at St Edmund Fishergate, where the first one was held, and the King's Centre, where the second one took place. I should also thank Nick Williams, the chair of the Trust, who has provided a Foreword for this volume; Susan Curran, a fellow trustee, who has again produced a volume of which the Trust may be proud; the authors, for agreeing to give papers at the conferences and for preparing them for publication; and my colleagues on the Trust, and also the Friends' group, for agreeing to support the conferences in the first place. Finally, as a conference with no audience has failed in its object, I wish to thank those who attended to hear the papers, and contributed to the discussions after they had been read. Some of these papers have been amended in the light of these discussions.

Dr Nicholas Groves is a trustee and the education officer of the Norwich Historic Churches Trust, and is a freelance lecturer and writer on church history. His previous publications have included The Medieval Churches of the City of Norwich *and* William Stephen Gilly: An exceptionally busy life, *the biography of a 19th-century clergyman.*

The publishers thank the Friends of the Norwich Historic Churches Trust for financial help towards the publication of this volume, all profits from which go to the Norwich Historic Churches Trust to help maintain Norwich's legacy of redundant medieval churches in the Trust's care. Thanks are also due to all those who kindly assisted with compiling the illustrations and gave permission for their work to be used. (Individual acknowledgements accompany the illustrations in the text.) Every effort has been made to obtain permission to reproduce work in copyright, but if any copyright material has inadvertently been reproduced without permission, the publishers will gladly remedy this omission.

Historic churches: heritage and voluntary action

Robert Piggott

Introduction

The 22 September 1852 issue of the *Morning Post* contained an article previewing the tenth Norwich Music Festival due to begin that evening.[1] After half a paragraph on the music to be expected at the event, the article then began to extol the many virtues of Norwich. On the subject of the streets of the city, it averred that they possess 'many advantages which are probably not to be found in any other English commercial city. We allude to the interesting specimens of ancient architecture – the antique churches – the picturesque continental-looking houses … the "plains" and charming gardens.'[2] It continues in this vein for some time, before providing a history of St Andrew's Hall and then a full column on the history of the cathedral. It's clear the author thought Norwich's historic buildings would prove a draw for readers. Similarly, in the *Observer*'s short 2007 piece on Norwich in its 'Let's all move to …' series, after the obligatory reference to Delia Smith, the author refers to Norwich's '[g]lorious, flint fronted medieval past; almost as many churches as coffee shops'.[3] Based on this very small sample – although I could also invoke writers such as Celia Fiennes or Daniel Defoe – we might argue that Norwich's medieval past, and in particular its historic ecclesiastical buildings, are central to the very idea of Norwich.

In relation to Edinburgh, Rebecca Madgin and Richard Rodger have shown that the idea (or more properly, myth) of Edinburgh as a non-industrial city was highly influential in planning decisions made by the city council, and led to the decline of what was formerly actually a fairly substantial manufacturing output.[4] This idea or 'spirit' of a place can be extremely influential in decision making by local authorities. In Norwich, the 1945 plan for post-war rebuilding focused on the city centre and encouraged care for Norwich's medieval heritage, including its churches.[5] Peter Townroe has argued that the 1967 *Draft Urban Plan for Norwich* came at a time of 'widespread public awareness' of Norwich's 'particularly rich heritage', which put pressure on the city council to address its various objectives for employment, retail and leisure 'within the constraints imposed by the height, mass, elevation, design and urban context of existing historic buildings'.[6] In this way the heritage of Norwich had become a public concern, and contributed to planning policy decisions in the city. Picking up on this observation, this paper focuses on the part voluntary action has played in protecting historic places of worship from demolition in Norwich, and thereby conserving the 'spirit of the place'.

The role of volunteers in the heritage sector has been recognized for some time now. Evidence to the House of Commons Culture, Media and Sport Committee 2006 report *Protecting and Preserving Our Heritage* widely applauded 'the huge contribution which [the voluntary and community sector make] to the restoration and management of the nation's heritage'.[7] This contribution is multifarious in a way which is typical of the voluntary sector more widely. I here examine some of the history of voluntary action in heritage-related practices by looking at historic places of worship in Norwich, and trying to set this in the context of the wider history of volunteering.

Places of worship and repair

Places of worship, like any building, require ongoing maintenance, but even with maintenance, processes of decay through the action of weather on materials used in construction may precipitate extensive structural repair at points in the lifespan of the building. This is perhaps particularly evident with churches in England, because of their longevity. Mortars will deteriorate and fail.[8] Structural movement, the action of the weather or the action of humans may cause some stone to crack or split.[9] Lead sheet roofing, often used as a covering for church roofs and highly durable, will need repair or replacement at some point in the life of the building – perhaps every 150 years – even if the structure is well maintained.[10] All of this implies that at some stage considerable costs will be incurred by those responsible for the management of these places, unless they favour ruination.

The longevity of church buildings and their various phases of repair, extension or 'restoration' are key elements of architectural history. But places of worship also serve to illustrate wider history. In Norwich, dedications to St Clement and St Olaf have been used to determine Danish influence on the town, and the Domesday Book mentions seven churches by name.[11] Norwich's medieval churches have provided important evidence for historians looking at the city, aiding calculations of population size[12] and providing evidence of prosperity and cultural life. On the latter point, in considering the spate of redevelopment of many parish churches in the 15th century, Jonathan Finch has argued that 'it is impossible not to see it as a regeneration of civic identity, since within the process were embedded the fortunes and aspirations of the city and its inhabitants'.[13]

The history of repair phases in the 20th and 21st centuries is no less important than this 15th-century phase, and it too helps to illuminate wider social processes. Part of this story concerns the development of outlets for voluntary action, although societal changes shaped by greater geographical mobility and suburban expansion, combined with changing attitudes to religious practice and to places of worship themselves, are also significant factors.

It is tempting to try to map the history of church building and church repair on to the history of voluntarism in England. There are certainly places where the story overlaps, but in the main provision of money for church repair cannot always be seen as voluntary action. In fact, there existed a common law obligation for parishioners to maintain the parish church, an obligation which was supervised by the ecclesiastical courts, backed with the threat of excommunication.[14] Notwithstanding this, we can see voluntary contribution to medieval churches as a vital element to their building economy. If a rector found himself unable to make provisions for the church in terms of texts, ritual equipment or repair, the parish was dependent on the resources of the laity to provide these things themselves.[15] In Norwich, the period of 15th-century rebuilding and expansion just mentioned was financed primarily through money from the living laity, as well as through bequests.[16] In the case of St Peter Mancroft, it has been suggested that its extensive rebuilding at this

Figure 1 Evidence of grant-aided repairs being carried out at St George Colegate, Norwich. (All photos by the author.)

time was to provide 'a civic alternative to the Cathedral Priory'.[17] Therefore, although seemingly obliged to keep these buildings in good repair, wealthy congregations chose to invest in their churches in a way which exceeded their obligations.

Norman Tanner has suggested that the ongoing popularity of bequests for the repair of churches in Norwich into the early 16th century demonstrates that the parishioners felt these places 'belonged to them'.[18] This is highly reminiscent of the way in which academic literature on the history of volunteering has stressed its role in civil society. In the words of Martin Daunton, '[v]oluntary associations created in the eighteenth and nineteenth centuries to provide hospitals and schools formed the basis of an active municipal culture from the middle of nineteenth century'.[19] In contributing to their parish church, we could say that medieval laity were engaged in active citizenship, supporting the provision of public services, and contributing to municipal culture in the same way that the creation of say the Foundling Hospital, which was paid for through subscription, contributed to the municipal culture of London in 1741.

The church rate and the rise of voluntarism

This story of voluntarism is tempered by the fact that for most people in medieval England Christianity was not a choice, and the Church had authority through its own courts to punish those failing to meet their Christian obligations.[20] The principle of taxation by the Church through tithes was not disputed, and the church calendar, alongside the agricultural cycle, would have dictated the 'English year'.[21] With the Elizabethan settlement, the parish became 'the basic unit of secular administration' and the parish vestry became the key site of local government, armed with tax-raising powers and elected officials in the form of churchwardens and overseers.[22] The parish church itself was, then, an office of government. The vestry's tax-raising powers included a form of local taxation levied on all ratepayers to meet the cost the repair of the nave, which as we have seen was their obligation in common law. This tax was known as the church rate.

In the 19th century, the church rate became a *cause célèbre* for dissenters aiming to overturn historic dishabilitation. In his exhaustive study of the parliamentary conflict surrounding the church rate question, J. P. Ellens has argued that this debate was central to the 'shaping [of] a secular and desacralized liberal state, and drawing Protestant Dissenters into the Liberal Party'.[23] Voluntaryism, which Ellens defines as 'free submission of the human will to the call of God', was common to both anti-Erastian Anglo-Catholics and Dissenters.[24] Ellens argues that '[t]his old Christian concern to maintain internal freedom for personal and congregational faith was translated into an ideology of voluntaryism after 1832 when Dissenters turned to politics and the state to force religiously based institutions, including places of worship and schools, to become free of state interference'.[25]

Gladstone's personal conversion from his 1838 work, *The State and its Relation to the Church*, in which he argued that the state and the church were divinely instituted and therefore natural allies, to his 1867 Compulsory Church Rate Abolition Bill which finally settled the church rate conflict, is indicative of the rising tide of voluntaryism in the second half of the 18th century.[26] Indeed, it has been said that late Victorians idealized a 'sphere of natural liberty' in which the private lives of individuals would be out of the reach of the state.[27] Their ideal, in the words of Jose Harris, was a 'neutral, passive, almost apolitical state' free of 'past entanglements with particularist interest groups'.[28] The battle against the church rate was a key conflict in the struggle for this ideal, a struggle against vested interests and against coercion by national government.

In Norwich, the strength of feeling associated with church rate conflict was exemplified not only in the case of St George Colegate, which witnessed prosecutions for non-payment of the rate in a case which was reported nationally, but also in the petitions in favour of keeping the rate presented to Parliament by the congregations of St John de Sepulchre and St Mark, Lakenham among others in the 1860s.[29] However, the strength of feeling against the rate in Norwich appears to have been high. In 1857 the *Ipswich Journal* reported a parliamentary return instigated by Lord Robert Cecil which showed that at one time or another the rate had been refused or had proved difficult to collect at St Benedict, St Clement, St Edmund, St Gregory, St James, St John Maddermarket, St Lawrence, St Margaret de Westwick, St Martin at Oak, St Michael at Thorn, St Swithin, St Paul and St George Colegate.[30] The members of the clergy completing the 1851 Church Census returns at the latter church and at St Mary Coslany both took the opportunity to lament the poor state of repair the refusal of a rate had meant for these buildings.[31]

Although Anglicans stuck to the legal principle of the church rate, it is arguable that the spirit of voluntaryism was not wholly confined to dissenters. Church building and repair did take place in Norwich in the 19th century, although Anglicans benefited from their relationship with the state. Thus, those who filled out the 1851 Church Census returns for

Figure 2 St James Pockthorpe, Norwich, now used as a puppet theatre

the Commissioners in relation to the new churches of Christ Church, New Catton and St Mark, Lakenham noted the combination of public and private funds that had resulted in their construction.[32] Meanwhile the assistant curate at St Martin at Palace took the opportunity of the Census to record the imminent restoration of the church, noting that £600 had been raised by subscription for the works.[33]

Further evidence of the spirit of voluntaryism comes in the shape of the Diocese of Norfolk's Diocesan Society for Building and Enlarging Churches, which began in 1836. The 1871 statement of accounts for the society claimed to have assisted 231 churches since its founding, with £4,433 10s having been distributed in grants of between £5 and £50, and a list of subscribers including clergy, persons styling themselves 'esquire' and a marquess.[34] Anglicans were however perhaps less successful than the dissenters in this area, with recurrent complaints that the funds of the Society were insufficient to meet the need.[35]

The mixed economy

In discussing voluntaryism, historians have often focused on the relationship between voluntary action and welfare provision. Geoffrey Finlayson's *Citizen, State and Social Welfare in Britain 1830–1990* is something of a core text for historians looking at the relationship between the state and welfare provision. In it, Finlayson criticized the over-emphasis on the role of the state in the delivery of welfare in Whiggish histories written after 1945. He argued that the history of welfare provision is not one of linearity, with increasing state provision at the expense of voluntary action, but one of 'recurrent experimentation' and '"shifting boundaries" between voluntarism and the state.'[36] Finlayson took the phrase 'the mixed economy of welfare' from social policy to describe sources of welfare which included not only the state, but also the family, neighbours, and organizations defined by voluntaryism, such as friendly societies, trade unions, penny savings banks, temperance societies, mechanics institutes and burial societies.[37]

Nineteenth-century voluntary organizations drew on centuries of thought on poor relief.[38] Growing fears of overpopulation combined in the latter part of the 18th century with the idea that those seeking welfare would be deprived of their independence if forced to rely on handouts.[39] In tandem, Evangelicals concerned with the inner life of the person focused their efforts and charitable works on the promotion of moral reform.[40] Increasingly, relief began to be raised from the poor themselves through such voluntary societies.[41] This was felt to be spiritually enriching and was considered to be 'self-help'.[42] As part of this, in the words of Donna Andrew, 'the role of philanthropist was transformed from being a donor of funds to becoming a donor of time and personal attention'.[43]

In the foregoing, we have seen a mixed economy of church building repair, in which government funds were supplemented by local giving, or where groups of subscribers banded together to provide services which, although strongly linked to government, were not under its centralized control. The Diocesan Society for Building and Enlarging Churches used the methods of charities: it was directed by a committee under the patronage of a member of the aristocracy, donating his time and good name, and produced a printed list of subscribers.[44] In its activities we can see the principle of self-help in operation, although this was somewhat ironically thrust upon the society rather than being freely chosen. The voluntary principle and a mixed economy for church repairs would continue to be important in the 20th century, but for different reasons. To understand these reasons we now turn to the story of changing attitudes to the parish church in the 19th century.

Church care

As well as its lists of subscribers and of grants given, the Diocesan Society's statement of accounts for 1871 contained the following note:

> The committee beg to suggest to those who are restoring Churches the careful preservation of remains of Ecclesiastical Art and Antiquities, even in cases where the remains cannot be used in restoration. In past days much that was interesting, as illustrating the history of Ecclesiastical Art in our country, has been recklessly destroyed; beautiful screens torn away and treated as mere lumber, poppy heads and other carvings of rich pattern, and ornamental iron work of elaborate design thrown aside, and antique fonts removed to some neighbouring rockery and replaced by new ones which have little to recommend them.

The fact that the committee needed to make this direction is illustrative of a mix of attitudes toward church buildings and their status in terms of sacredness or as buildings of historic interest. Richard Morris has argued that '[t]he Church of England maintained the

Figure 3 St Martin at Palace, Norwich (now redundant and between tenants)

theory of the church as a holy place through the eighteenth century, but did so without much conviction .... By 1800 this belief in the intrinsic sanctity of an ecclesiastical site was all but dead.'[45] He went on to say that '[t]he fact that it exists today is largely due to the efforts of the ritualists and the Camdenians in the 1840s'.[46]

Figure 4 Funded by the National Lottery: St George Tombland, Norwich (still in operation as a parish church)

Stuart Piggott tied the concern for ritual of the Oxford Movement to the rise of archaeological societies in the 1840s.[47] As he put it:

[i]n turning the attention of the parson, the squire, and the churchwardens to the structure and fabric of their church, the movement injected a stiff dose of medieval archaeology and architectural history into the clerical and lay population of parish after parish.[48]

While recognizing this, we should note that an interest in the history of their parish had been a pastime of many members of the clergy over the previous century, as Rosemary Sweet has shown.[49] In Norfolk this is exemplified by the activities of the rector of Fersfield, Francis Blomefield, who compiled a parish-by-parish history of the county, published in 1739, and expanded by the rector of Oxburgh, Charles Parkin, following Blomefield's death.[50] This antiquarian interest continued in Norwich in the 19th century with the founding in the 1840s of the Norfolk and Norwich Archaeological Association, with the majority of the committee made up of clergy and the subscription kept low, apparently in order to encourage improvement among churchwardens.[51]

However, not everyone in the Church of England was seized by an enthusiasm for historic places. The belief in the sanctity of a church building (or its possibility of removal) was a point of conflict both within the Church of England and between the Church and

Figure 5 St Peter Hungate, Norwich

conservationists. Ben Weinstein has illuminated this disagreement with reference to the City of London's Wren churches. Faced with the decline of the residential population in the City as it transformed into a centre of commerce, a Union of Benefices Act (1860) was passed which allowed for a church to be demolished, and its plot to be sold to fund the construction of a church building in the suburbs.[52] Weinstein has argued that the cause of the 'demolitionists' was firmly rooted in an Evangelical theology, 'keen to revive the Church of England through urban missionary work and the remobilization of church resources'.[53] This issue was then one that divided evangelicals from anglo-catholics. It was also one of the founding causes of the Society for the Protection of Ancient Buildings (SPAB), with William Morris (himself exposed to high church anglicanism during his time at Marlborough College)[54] writing to *The Times* in 1878 lamenting their ongoing destruction.[55]

The debate between the conservationists and the 'demolitionists' in the Church of England was not confined to the 19th century, although it took on an emotional resonance which was presumably not present in the utilitarian rationalizing undertaken by evangelicals that Weinstein describes. Evidence contributed to the 1995 report *Spirit of Place: Redundant Churches as Urban Resources* suggested that to a church's congregation, who had developed an emotional attachment to the building, '[c]losure can often feel like failure, and a church's former congregation may prefer the clarity and completeness [that demolition] offers'. The report quoted one diocesan officer as saying that 'nobody wants to walk into a furniture warehouse and say "That's where I was married"'.[56]

Even as the conservationist's powers grew, churches remained outside of the reach of the nascent heritage protection legislation, with 'ecclesiastical exemption' being granted from the 1913 Ancient Monuments Consolidation and Amendment Act.[57] The Union of Benefices laws were updated in the 20th century by an Act in 1919 and then by Measures in 1921 and 1923 under the new dispensation inaugurated by the Church Assemblies Act (1919). Although the 1923 Measure established that proposals to demolish a church had to be put before both Houses of Parliament. and the advice of the Royal Fine Art Commission had to be sought to 'protect churches of "archaeological, historic or artistic interest"',[58] it was not until the Town and Country Planning Acts of 1944 and 1947 that ecclesiastical buildings could be listed and so become a material consideration in the determination of planning applications.[59] When listed building controls were introduced in 1968, the ecclesiastical exemption from listed building consent remained, with dioceses managing the Church of England's own faculty jurisdiction to control works to the church, its contents and the churchyard.[60]

Following the Second World War, the Church of England introduced the Reorganisation of Areas Measure (1944), to deal with administrative issues related to churches that had been destroyed during the war.[61] It also began to investigate redundancy, setting up a committee in 1948 under the chairmanship of the bishop of Norwich, Percy Herbert. His committee found that 400 churches were 'seldom or never used', of which 300 were of 'architectural or historic interest'.[62] Between 1948 and 1958, 'some 230 churches were demolished, many as the result of war damage or comprehensive redevelopment'.[63] In 1952, partly at the behest of the Pilgrim's Trust and the Society of Antiquaries, the Church set up the Historic Churches Preservation Trust to begin to address what it had estimated as a £4 million backlog of repairs.[64]

In 1958 a new Commission began its work under the chairmanship of Lord Bridges. Reporting in 1960, it called for an improved procedure for redundancy and for funds to be made available for those buildings that it was felt warranted preservation.[65] It was in response to the Bridges report[66] that the Pastoral Measure (1968) and the Redundant Churches and Other Religious Buildings Act (1969) were devised.

In introducing the Pastoral Measure to the Church Assembly, the bishop of Chester, Gerald Ellison, argued that 'the powers taken to meet the needs of reorganisation as a result of war damage [were] now found to be needed for wider application'.[67] As the name suggests, the Pastoral Measure was largely concerned with administrative issues related to the cure of souls. The effect this would have on church buildings appears to have been more or less a side issue. On this point the bishop remarked:

> [t]he Church has a heavy enough burden to bear in keeping in good condition the churches which are needed for parochial purposes, and you will readily understand that church people are reluctant to spend much needed funds in keeping in repair buildings which are no longer needed for public worship.

To this end the Redundant Churches Fund was set up, with the 1969 Act putting government grants to the Fund on a legal footing, and maintaining the ecclesiastical exemption by excluding redundant church buildings from section 40 of the 1968 Town and Country Planning Act, which prohibited the demolition of listed buildings.

Figure 6 St Gregory, Norwich, now an antiques centre

Norwich

In 1967 Percy Herbert's successor as bishop of Norwich, Launcelot Fleming, appointed a commission of his own in the city to examine the issues the diocese faced. These were similar to those faced by the Diocese of London earlier in the century. Although the city of Norwich grew in geographical area in the 20th century, household size decreased, meaning that it grew only very slowly in population.[68] The change in the pattern of residential population was particularly marked in the parish of Coslany, which had a population of 7,000 in 1841, but only 300 in 1971.[69] This was exacerbated by the ongoing decline in public worship and its effect on Anglican congregation size. One measure of this is baptisms per live thousand births, which had begun to decline nationally in 1950 from 672 per thousand that year to 466 per thousand in 1970.[70]

The Norwich Commission, led by Henry, Lord Brooke of Cumnor (a Conservative peer) reported near the beginning of 1970, and declared 24 of Norwich's churches to be surplus to requirements.[71] This prompted the Norwich Society to call for a group to be formed to save these buildings from demolition,[72] as although the majority of the medieval churches in Norwich had been listed in 1954, their demolition would have been legally permissible under the 1969 Act. Although the Redundant Churches Fund had been established by that Act, the Act had set the maximum contribution by the government to the fund in the initial five-year period at £200,000.[73]

At a public meeting called in October 1970 to form the Friends of Norwich Historic Churches, the lord mayor of Norwich, John Jarrold, spoke of the possibility of £100,000 needing to be raised over the following ten years.[74] Speaking in a House of Lords debate in 1972, Lord Brooke suggested that even if the Redundant Churches Fund could have covered the costs, 'it seemed to us that the primary responsibility lay with the people of Norwich to seek to find means to preserve their own heritage'.[75] The Fund, now the Churches Conservation Trust, did bear some of the brunt, however, taking on three churches – St John Maddermarket, St Lawrence and (in 2000) St Augustine.

In his report on volunteering in 1948, William Beveridge looked to what he called the 'spirit of service' which was in 'our people'.[76] However, he argued that, 'only in the few is it the driving force that makes them pioneers'.[77] Beveridge argued that these few 'call it forth in others; they create the institutions and societies through which it acts; they lead by their example'.[78] If he was right, then in Norwich a likely candidate for this 'few', with the time and inclination to take up the cause of saving the city's churches, was Lady Wilhelmina (Billa) Harrod. She had worked for the Georgian Group in the 1930s and was a member of the Norfolk Branch of the Council for Protection of Rural England.[79]

Lady Harrod called on her friend Sir John Betjeman to speak at the October meeting, which would launch the group Friends of Norwich Churches. She acted as chair for the group at the start, and presided over this first meeting.[80] That meeting was timed to coincide with an exhibition held at St Michael at Plea, with the title 'Investment in the Future', run jointly by the City Council, the Norwich Society, the Mousehold Heath Conservators and the Norfolk Association of Architects.[81]

For the exhibition the architects 'produced plans for the adaptation of five disused churches – one into a hostel for students, another into a shelter for vagrants, another into a regimental museum, another into a refectory, and another into a community centre for the people of the new houses and flats surrounding it'.[82] This was indicative of the strategy of adaptive reuse adopted by the charity the Norwich Historic Churches Trust, which succeeded the Friends of Norwich Churches group and registered as a charity in 1974.[83] The trust was established with the objective of 'preservation and maintenance for the public benefit of redundant churches of all denominations in the City of Norwich, which are of historic or architectural value' to 'let or hire as the trustees see fit'.[84] It was supported by an annual grant of £20,000 from the city council up until 1995, since when it has relied on rents, voluntary giving and grant aid from other sources, such as English Heritage and the Heritage Lottery Fund.[85]

By June 1971 the Friends had gained 300 members and had raised £3,000, which was spent on repairs to the tower at St Michael at Plea and repairing the buttress at St Gregory.[86] Lady Harrod had become the vice-chair, with the former chairman of Colman's, W. Rowan Hare, taking on the chairmanship.[87] Harrod was beginning to turn her attentions to Norfolk's rural churches, which although in use were seeing dwindling congregations, and were without state support. To this end she organized the publication of *Norfolk County Churches and the Future*, published by the Norfolk Society in 1972. It comprised short articles by a variety of authors. In his foreword Launcelot Fleming's successor as bishop of Norwich, Maurice Wood, hedged his bets between the demolitionists, whom he called 'church-plant rationalisers' and the conservationists ('village church preservationists'), arguing that the booklet would 'make a significant contribution to this urgent ongoing debate'.[88]

The Conservative MP Patrick Cormack, who contributed to the *Norfolk County Churches and the Future,* had submitted a private member's bill calling on Parliament to 'make further provision for the preservation of churches and other ecclesiastical buildings of historic and architectural importance' the previous year.[89] Like so many other private member's bills it did not become law, but Cormack was encouraged that time had been allowed for public debate on the issue, and argued that the government agreed it held a national responsibility to maintain historic places of worship.[90] However, despite championing state aid, Cormack was keen to reinforce the principle of self-help: 'It is no part of my intention that Government or local authorities should provide cushions for negligent incumbents or for lazy congregations, or that we should stifle the voluntary appeal.'[91] Lady Harrod's son Dominick, at the time the BBC's economics correspondent, used his article in the booklet to give advice to parochial church councils on how such money could be raised, listing church fetes, postcards, brass rubbing and leaflets on the church as possible sources of income.[92]

State aid for historic places of worship in use was not granted until 1977.[93] The secretary of state for the environment, Peter Shore, reported to parliament in October that year that he had made £250,000 available for the financial year to deal with urgent repairs, with a further £750,000 in the following year, rising to £2 million in 1979–80.[94] The practice continued into the next decade, and after its formation in 1983 English Heritage took up management of the scheme.[95] In 1996 the money began to be drawn from the Heritage Lottery Fund (HLF), but the scheme continued to be administered by English Heritage. This arrangement continued until 2012, when the HLF took on administration, retaining English Heritage's (now Historic England) technical expertise.[96]

English Heritage generally gave grant aid at a figure below 80 per cent of the cost of the works, leaving a proportion of the total needing to be raised by the applicant, which in the case of the Church of England was the parochial church council. Matched funding by applicants decreased to 5 per cent for projects under £1 million in the successor scheme, although the scheme stipulates that a proposal must 'include works that help the heritage of your place of worship to be more widely understood'[97] rather than simply repair the building, and so maintains the voluntary principle in a different way. In Norwich, between 2005 and 2011 English Heritage provided grant aid to fund repair works at Christ Church, New Catton; St Mark, Lakenham; and St George, Tombland.[98] As part of the successor scheme, the HLF have awarded grant aid again to St George, Tombland and to St George, Colegate.[99]

The mixed economy of heritage

I have tried to demonstrate the convergences between the history of repairing places of worship and the history of voluntary organizations. Organizations such as the Norwich and Norfolk Churches Trusts and parochial church councils continue to use methods developed hundreds of years before, such as subscription, committee direction and opportunities for association (such as Norfolk Churches Trust annual bike ride or the church fete), just as voluntary organizations did in the 19th century. This includes aristocratic patronage, which was a feature of the Diocesan Society for Church Building and of the Norfolk Historic Churches Trust.[100]

In the 20th and 21st centuries the voluntary sector has been forced to adapt to the increased reach of the state. This can be seen from the appointment of the director general of voluntary organisations during the First World War to the Blair government's Office of the Third Sector.[101] Not all voluntary organizations became clients of the state over this period, but an increasing willingness by some to take on this role is evident.[102] Geoffrey Finlayson suggested that this is because the realization dawned that 'the state could not cope with all the demands that were made on it, and required to make use of the resources of the voluntary sector'.[103] Therefore, some element of dependency of the state on voluntary organizations has developed. This has been evident in the mixed economy of historic building repair, which itself is evidence of a mixed economy of heritage more generally. In achieving the policy objectives of maintenance of historic fabric, or improved understanding of history, the state, through agencies such as the HLF or Historic England, has been dependent on voluntary organizations to meet its goals.

This relationship has been one of mutual dependence, however, with heritage managed at a local level but taking advantage of national trends. We have seen this in the rise of grant aid funding for historic buildings. This has been available to redundant places of worship in Norwich too. Since 2005 the Norwich Historic Churches Trust has received grant aid from English Heritage for repair projects at St Michael Coslany, St John de Sepulchre and St Martin at Palace Plain.[104] In the 1980s many churches across the country benefited from repair work carried out by the Manpower Services Commission.[105] At least one former church in Norwich, St James, Pockthorpe, used labour provided through this scheme in its conversion to a puppet theatre in 1980.[106]

In the 21st century the Labour government invested a large amount of money in 'capacity building'. This was largely targeted at improving voluntary organizations' abilities to raise money. For places of worship in use, English Heritage launched the Inspired! campaign in 2006. One element was to appoint advisors to denominations 'to help denominations help themselves'.[107] This translated into support officers paid partly by dioceses and partly by English Heritage.[108] The strategy of capacity building has continued to the present day, with the HLF granting Norwich Historic Churches Trust £9,300 to improve the fundraising skills of its volunteers, trustees and staff in 2013.[109]

Concluding remarks

In conclusion, let us return to St George, Colegate, the most high-profile case in the church rate conflict in Norwich. In their fight for the voluntary principle, the rate payers may actually have contributed to the survival of the Georgian interior, which provides some of its historic interest. St George was awarded £85,900 by the HLF in 2014 to pay for repairs. As we have seen such grant aid is normally given on the proviso that the church would engage with the public, which will help, in the words of the HLF, 'to increase the number of people who take an active interest in celebrating these historic buildings and who will care for them in the future'.[110] I understand that for St George this will mean a heritage trail telling the stories of the merchants associated with the church in the Georgian period.[111]

As we saw, in founding the Norfolk and Norwich Archaeological Society the clergy of Norfolk were interested merely in improving the tastes of churchwardens. We can see the activities promoted by the HLF as having a much wider import, with the calculation that if they can widen the appeal of historic buildings by focusing on the human stories attached to them, then a greater number are likely to be interested in conserving the buildings for the future. This policy objective is delivered at a local level, through the activities of volunteers. For this reason, even though much of the money comes from centralized sources, the mixed economy of heritage requires a remarkable amount of voluntary action. Whether it is the art student giving her time one day a week to invigilate in a redundant church, the vicar abseiling down the tower, the local person lending their time on a heritage open day, or the PCC member auctioning off the hole in the church roof on eBay, voluntary action is vital to the conservation of historic buildings.

Robert Piggott is a PhD researcher based at the University of Huddersfield. His article in this collection forms part of his research for his PhD thesis which concerns aspects of church building and repair in the modern period. This project is part of an AHRC funded initiative, the Heritage Consortium, coordinated by the History Department at the University of Hull. Prior to commencing his PhD, he worked for English Heritage (now Historic England) for a number of years.

Notes

1. Anon., 'Norwich musical festival', *Morning Post,* 22 September 1852.
2. Ibid.
3. Tom Dyckoff, 'Lets all move to… Norwich', *Observer,* 25 March 2007.
4. R. Madgin and R. Rodger, 'Inspiring capital', Urban History Vol. 40, Issue 3 (August 2013), pp. 507–29.
5. P. Townroe 'Norwich since 1945', in C. Rawcliffe and R. Wilson (eds), *Norwich since 1550*, London and New York: Hambledon and London, 2004.
6. Ibid., p. 490.
7. Culture, Media and Sport Committee, *Protecting and Preserving Our Heritage,* 12 July 2006, HC 912-I, para 115.
8. See English Heritage, *Practical Building Conservation: Mortars, renders and plasters,* 2011, pp. 122–63.
9. See English Heritage, *Stone Masonry, English Heritage research transactions: research and case studies in architectural conservation,* 1990, pp. 2–3.
10. See English Heritage, *Metals, English Heritage research transactions: research and case studies in architectural conservation,* 1993 pp. 93–109.
11. B. Ayers, 'The urban environment', in Rawcliffe and Wilson (2004), pp. 5–9.

12 See Ibid., pp.19–20.
13 J. Finch, 'The churches', in Rawcliffe and Wilson (2004), p. 49.
14 J. P. Ellens, *Religious Routes to Gladstonian Liberalism: the church rate conflict in England and Wales, 1832–68*, University Park, Pa.: Pennsylvania State University Press, 1994, p. 12.
15 Ibid,. p. 57.
16 Ibid., p. 60.
17 Ibid., p. 63.
18 N. Tanner, *The Church in Late Medieval Norwich*, Toronto, Ont.: Pontifical Institute of Mediaeval Studies, 1984, p. 126.
19 M. Daunton, *Trusting Leviathan: The politics of taxation in Britain 1793–1914*, Cambridge: Cambridge University Press, 2001, 2007, p. 25.
20 See D. Rosman, *The Evolution of the English Churches 1500–2000,* Cambridge: Cambridge University Press, 2003, 2011, pp. 12–13.
21 Ibid., p. 14 and S. Roud, *The English Year*, London: Penguin, 2006.
22 D. Eastwood, *Government and Community in the English Provinces*, Basingstoke: Macmillan, 1997, p. 19.
23 Ellens (1994), p. 1.
24 Ibid., p. 2.
25 Ibid.
26 See ibid., pp. 5–6 and pp. 223–54.
27 Jose Harris, *Private Lives, Public Spirit: Britain 1870–1914*, London: Penguin, 1994, p. 183.
28 Ibid., p. 184; but also see Eastwood (1997), esp. ch. 6.
29 Anon., 'House of Commons – Thursday', *Standard*, 3 February 1860, p. 2.; Anon., 'Tuesday 28 April', *Ipswich Journal,* 2 May 1863.
30 Anon., 'Church rates', *Ipswich Journal*, 7 February 1857.
31 See J. Ede and N. Virgoe, *Religious Worship in Norfolk*, Norfolk: Norfolk Record Society, 1998, pp. 123, 124. See also C. Binfield, 'Church and chapel', in Rawcliffe and Wilson (2004), pp. 409–36.
32 Ede and Virgoe (1998), pp. 121, 135.
33 Ibid., p. 129.
34 Norfolk Records Office, DN/DAB2.
35 See ibid. and Anon 'Norwich Diocesan Church Building Society', *Ipswich Journal*, 1 May 1883.
36 G. Finlayson, *Citizen, State and Social Welfare in Britain 1830–1990*, Oxford and New York: Clarendon Press, 1994, p.18.
37 Ibid., pp. 6–7 and ch. 1.
38 See D. Andrew, *Philanthropy and Police*, Princeton, N.J.: Princeton University Press, 1990.
39 Ibid., pp, 135–62.
40 Ibid., pp. 165–74. See also M. J. D. Roberts, *Making English Morals: Voluntary associations and moral reform in England 1787–1886*, Cambridge: Cambridge University Press, 2004.
41 Andrew (1990), p. 201.
42 See Finlayson (1994), pp. 76–80.
43 Andrew (1990), p. 201.
44 See ibid., pp. 49, 57.
45 R. Morris, *Churches in the Landscape*, London: J. M. Dent, 1989, p. 450.
46 Ibid.
47 S. Piggott, *Ruins in a Landscape*, Edinburgh: University Press, 1976, pp. 175–6.
48 Ibid., p. 176.
49 R. Sweet, *Antiquaries: The discovery of the past in eighteenth century Britain*, London: Hambledon and London, 2004.

50 S. Wade-Martins, *The Conservation Movement in Norfolk*, Martlesham: Boydell & Brewer, 2015 pp. 26–7.
51 Ibid., p. 35.
52 B. Weinstein, 'Questioning a late Victorian "dyad": preservationism, demolitionism, and the City of London Churches, 1860–1904', *Journal of British Studies*, Vol. 53 Issue 2, April 2014.
53 Ibid., p. 403.
54 See F. MacCarthy, *William Morris: A life for our time*, London: Faber, 1994, pp. 43–5.
55 W. Morris, 'Destruction of City churches', letter to *The Times*, 17 April 1878.
56 Comedia, *Spirit of Place: Redundant churches as urban resources,* Stroud: Comedia, 1995, pp. 29, 34.
57 See J. Delafons, *Politics and Preservation*, London: E. & F. N. Spon, 1997, p. 119.
58 Ibid., p. 121.
59 See ibid., p. 119.
60 See ibid., p. 120.
61 Ecclesiastical Committee, Ninetieth Report, 1944 HL15 HC45.
62 Delafons (1997), p. 121.
63 Ibid.
64 National Churches Trust, *Keeping Churches Alive*, 2013, p. 3.
65 Ibid., p. 123.
66 And to the Paul Report, which looked at 'the payment and deployment of clergy', Lord Bishop of Chester, HL Deb., 13 May 1968, vol. 292, cc. 2–25, para. 4.
67 Ibid.
68 See Peter Townroe, 'Norwich since 1945' in Rawcliffe and Wilson (2004), p. 472.
69 Ibid., p. 477.
70 G. Davie, *Religion in Britain: a persistent paradox*, Hoboken, N.J.: John Wiley, 2015, p. 50.
71 Anon., 'Norwich churches', *Eastern Daily Press*, 28 June 1970.
72 John Cornforth, 'Must all the country churches go? II', *Country Life*, 27 August 1970, p. 504.
73 Redundant Churches and Other Religious Buildings Act 1969, s.1(2).
74 Anon., 'Friends' fight for churches praised', *Eastern Daily Press*, 29 October 1970.
75 HL Deb., 18 April 1972, vol. 330, cc. 18–52, para. 42.
76 W. Beveridge, 'Co-ordination and the spirit of service', in *Voluntary Action: A Report on Methods of Social Advance*, London: G. Allen & Unwin, 1948.
77 Ibid.
78 Ibid.
79 See Mark Girouard, 'Obituary: Billa Harrod', *Independent*, 12 May 2005, p. 38 and Anon., 'Lady Harrod, campaigner for Norfolk's churches and long-term friend and confidante of Sir John Betjeman', *Daily Telegraph*, 12 May 2005, p. 25.
80 Cornforth (1970), p. 504; 'Friends' fight …' (1970).
81 Jonathan Mardle (aka Eric Fowler), 'The salvation of Norwich', *Eastern Daily Press*, 14 October 1970.
82 Ibid.
83 Norwich Historic Churches Trust, Trustees' Report and Financial Statements, 2014, p. 2.
84 Ibid.
85 Comedia (1995), p. 53; Norwich Historic Churches Trust, Trustees' Report and Financial Statements, 2014, p. 17.
86 'Norwich churches' (1971).
87 Ibid.
88 Norfolk Society, *Norfolk County Churches and the Future*, Holt: Norfolk Society Committee for County Churches, 1972.

89 HC Deb., 21 December 1971, vol. 828, c. 1318.
90 Norfolk Society (1972), p. 20.
91 Ibid., p. 21.
92 Ibid., p. 19.
93 Delafons (1997), p. 124.
94 HC Deb., 26 October 1977, vol. 936, c. 863W.
95 See HC Deb., 19 December 1988, vol. 144, cc. 235–55, and HC Deb., 18 December 1996, vol. 287, cc. 913–19.
96 G. Braithwaite, 'Maintaining the legacy', *Conservation Bulletin*, no. 61, 2009, p. 23; English Heritage Annual Report and Accounts, 2013.
97 Heritage Lottery Fund, 'Grants for places of worship: application guidance', December 2013, p. 5.
98 Anon., 'Big cash boost for church roof', *Eastern Daily Press*, 7 July 2007; Anon., 'Churches to receive £7 million in repair grants', *Daily Telegraph*, 3 July 2008; David Bale, 'Essential repairs needed at 13th century Norwich church', *Eastern Daily Press*, 29 April 2014.
99 www.hlf.org.uk/about-us/media-centre/press-releases/east-england-churches-full-joys-spring-thanks-lottery-grant (accessed 25 September 2015).
100 Aristocratic patronage was a key feature of charities in the Victorian and Edwardian eras. See Harris (1994), p. 188.
101 See P. Grant, 'Voluntarism and the impact of the First World War' and P. Alcock, 'Voluntary action, New Labour, and the 'third sector' – in M. Hilton and J. McKay (eds), *The Ages of Voluntarism: How we got to the Big Society*, Oxford: Oxford University Press, 2011.
102 See Finlayson (1994), pp. 287–93.
103 Ibid. p. 352.
104 Norwich Historic Churches Trust, Trustees' Report and Financial Statements, 2012, p. 16; Trustees' Report and Financial Statements, 2010, p.16.
105 See E. Filby, 'Faith, charity and citizenship', in Hilton and McKay (2011).
106 *Look East: Puppet Theatre*, 1980, Norwich: East Anglian Film Archive, www.eafa.org.uk/catalogue/216736 (accessed 24 September 2015).
107 English Heritage, Inspired! 2006.
108 See https://historicengland.org.uk/advice/caring-for-heritage/places-of-worship/support-officers/ (accessed 24 September 2015).
109 See www.norwich-churches.org/PDFs/Press_Release_051113_lottery_funding_LQ.pdf (accessed 25 September 2015).
110 www.hlf.org.uk/about-us/media-centre/press-releases/east-england-churches-full-joys-spring-thanks-lottery-grant (accessed 25 September 2015).
111 Pers. comm. from volunteer at St George Colegate.

The use, reuse and abuse of 'alternative use': a historical perspective on the reappropriation of urban closed churches for other purposes

Steven Saxby

'Alternative use' is the technical term for one of the three options permissible under the legislation that has governed the closure of Church of England churches since 1969.[1] From 1969 to 2010, a total of 1,795 closure schemes were made. Other than the 10 per cent of schemes related to part-demolition, the sale of sites, and pending future use, 19 per cent of schemes led to preservation, 20 per cent to demolition and, by far the largest number, 51 per cent, to alternative use.[2] With these figures in mind – and with the impression created by alternative use in urban centres like Norwich, York and a few other places – it is easy to forget that the use of Anglican churches solely for purposes other than regular public worship in England is a relatively new phenomenon, and that the path towards it, as well as the experience of wider alternative use for the first 45 years following 1969, was not without controversy. This paper therefore considers the history of developments which led to alternative use becoming a category of church closure. It also considers some of the history surrounding the use, reuse and perceived abuse of 'alternative use'. Finally, it points to some recent developments in church closure policy which may affect the future of alternative use, if not the future of church closure in general.

That churches throughout the history of England were used for other purposes in addition to worship is not in dispute, but the appropriation of churches solely for purposes other than worship is a comparatively recent development. Church closure is nothing new. It is clear that even before the Reformation churches did close or fall into disuse, and were either taken down or allowed to go to ruin. In Norwich there was St Michael Conesford, for example, which Nicholas Groves in *The Medieval Churches of the City of Norwich* states was subsumed into the precinct of the Austin Friars before it was demolished in 1360 to allow for the building of a cloister.[3] Other closures included those allowed by Henry VIII's Union of Contiguous Benefices Act 1545[4] (which made it possible to unite any two churches less than a mile apart if one was worth less than £6 per year), as well as those under special Acts of Parliament secured for planned closures at York in 1547, Lincoln in 1549 and soon after in Stamford, Chipping Ongar and Rochester.[5] Churches closed under these Acts were either demolished or abandoned, as were many in Norfolk, Essex and elsewhere.[6] Abandoned churches were put to other uses – as, for example, was the Saxon church of St Peter on the Wall at Bradwell, which was used as a barn for the storage of grain and cattle from the mid-18th century until its restoration as a place of worship in 1920[7] – but such uses were opportunist rather than planned or endorsed by the Church.

At the beginning of the 19th century, no closure of an Anglican parish church was

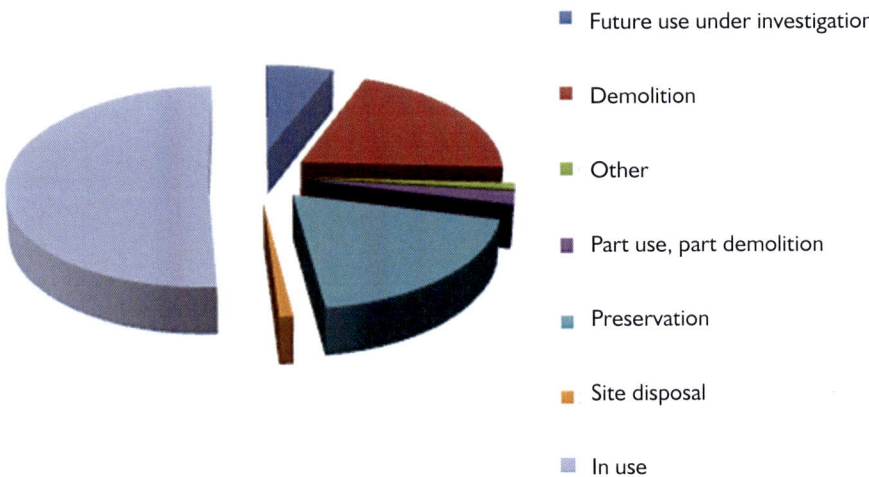

Figure 1 Categories for main future use of churches with closure schemes agreed by the Church Commissioners

Data source: Linda Monkton, *Churches and Closure in the Church of England: A Summary Report* (London: English Heritage, 2010).

possible without an Act of Parliament. Fifty-one churches had been rebuilt or repaired in the City of London after the Great Fire of 1666, and pressure to close some of them began to mount in the 1830s. St Christopher le Stocks had been demolished by an Act of Parliament in 1782 to extend the Bank of England,[8] and the demolition of St Michael, Crooked Lane in 1831, to create King William Street as a wider approach to London Bridge,[9] gave Richard Lambert Jones (1783–1863), an influential member of the Corporation of London, the idea of pulling down more churches in order to make further improvements to the City.[10] A committee of the Corporation was formed in 1833, with Lambert Jones as its chairperson. Even though the archbishop of Canterbury, William Howley (1766–1848), and the bishop of London, Charles James Blomfield (1786–1857), approved of the plans, they later withdrew their support following opposition in the press.[11] Yet these were the origins of Church of England church closure policy, for Blomfield returned to the idea of planning the closure of City of London churches in the 1850s with proposals that were not only shaped by the proposals first made in the 1830s but were to shape the Union of Benefices Bill of 1860, which when approved was the first piece of modern legislation under which churches, albeit only in London, were closed without recourse to a separate Act of Parliament for each closure.

From Blomfield's attempts in the 1850s onwards, the prospect of alternative use was raised but it was not actually permitted until 1923, and then only for educational, charitable or other purposes associated with the Church of England, until wider alternative use was allowed for war-damaged areas from 1944 and nationwide from 1952. So for nearly a hundred years, in which the principle of closing churches was championed by some within the institutional Church of England, alternative use as it exists today was resisted by opponents from within the church hierarchy and beyond. Provisions for use by non-English speaking Anglicans were made in the bills for church closure put before

Figure 2 Plaque on the site of St Michael Conesford, Norwich, demolished in 1360. Photo courtesy of Simon Knott, http://www.norfolkchurches.co.uk/norwichmichaelconesford/norwichmichael conesford.htm

parliament in the 1850s, but the original text of the 1860 bill went further in suggesting that surplus churches might be used not only for Anglican services in Welsh or Irish – or any foreign language[12] – but also by Protestant dissenters. This was too much for the evangelical bishop of Oxford, Samuel Wilberforce (1805–1873), who argued successfully against his Broad Church episcopal colleagues, that the clause allowing this should be struck out:

> The Socinians of North America and the Mormons of the Salt Lake District would be entitled to come in under this uninhabited churches clause. It would be found to be impossible to deal with various sects drawing distinctions so nicely as to admit one and leave out another. The effect of this clause would be to open a door to principles which, if carried to their legitimate extent, would sanction the conclusions of those who claimed the churches as the common property of all sects and denominations of religion.[13]

Figure 3 St Peter on the Wall, Bradwell, a Saxon church used as a barn from the mid-18th century and restored as a place of worship in 1920. Image from Wikimedia Commons, https://upload.wikimedia.org/wikipedia/commons/5/58/St_Peter-on-the-Wall.jpg

Figure 4 St Michael Crooked Lane, London, demolished in 1831.
Picture from http://london.lovesguide.com/michael_crooked.htm, courtesy of Dickon Love.

This marks a clear difference from how alternative use was regarded after 1969, when use by other denominations became normative, and use by other faiths became possible. Considering the number of Anglican churches now used by Orthodox and other nonconformist congregations, it is significant that in 1860, the bishops in the Lords amended the bill to clarify that closed churches should not be used by the Greek Orthodox,[14] and that five years later, Sir Samuel Morton Peto (1809–1889), a prominent Baptist member of parliament for the Liberals – including for Norwich between 1847 and 1854 – felt it necessary to try to calm fears that nonconformist bodies were seeking to purchase Anglican churches subject to closure.[15]

Thus until 1923 church closure effectively equalled demolition, and without a separate Act of Parliament was only possible under the Union of Benefices Act 1860 in London. It was principally a means by which the resources of churches in the inner districts of London could be used to build new churches in areas of growing population in greater

Figure 5
The site today of Holy Trinity Minories, Aldgate. Photo from http://london.lovesguide.com/holytrinity_minories.htm, courtesy of Dickon Love.

London. Repeated attempts from the 1860s onwards to secure similar legislation for other urban areas, not least Norwich, Lincoln and Exeter, continued to fail until the advent of the national provisions contained first in the Union of Benefices Measure 1923. Without elaborating on the complexities of the debates surrounding church closure in the second half of the 19th century, it was clearly the case that the main incentive for those seeking church closure was to use it as a means to fund more churches elsewhere, and the main opposition, which grew throughout the period, related to the increasing regard for the heritage value of churches. It is also safe to say that the concept of alternative use hardly featured in the debate.

That said, some of the issues that were to arise in relation to the alternative use of churches were raised in relation to the alternative use of church sites. Many were appalled by the prospect of the site of a demolished church being put to secular purposes, with frequent anxieties expressed about any activities related to alcohol taking place on the site of a former church. For example, when Edward Nugent (1835–1890) the sixth earl of Milltown, attempted to overturn the 1860 Act in 1885, he said – in relation to the planned closure of Holy Trinity Minories, where a large number of persons had been interred – that 'it was impossible to exaggerate the immense amount of decaying humanity which really constituted the soil' and would have to be disturbed if some 'gin palace or a warehouse were erected in place of the church'.[16] At a church congress in 1894, W. Digby Thurnam, an ecclesiastical lawyer of Lincoln's Inn, put the case more strongly:

> It is idle to pretend that these houses of God are useless. Is not the better plan to use them, as their pious founders desired, as the terms of their consecration declared? A more excellent way might surely be found than to sell them for banks, building societies, and breweries, literally turning the Father's house into a house of merchandise, if not into a den of thieves.[17]

That church closure meant demolition is evident not only in the provisions of the 1860 Act but also in the only two Acts of Parliament before 1923 which provided for the closure of a number of churches at once in particular urban areas. The Liverpool and Wigan Churches Act of 1904 and the Manchester Churches Act of 1906 were both explicit that any purchaser of the churches identified for closure would be required to demolish them within specified periods.[18]

Yet the early 20th century saw the emergence of sympathy towards the idea of alternative use. Perhaps this was helped by a couple of prominent churches being put to other purposes in the late 19th century. In 1882 St Matthew Spring Gardens, albeit only a chapel of ease to St Martin in the Fields but in a prominent location near to Trafalgar Square, was acquired by the Ministry of Woods and Forests following the passing of the Public Offices Site Act, which provided for enlargements to the Admiralty,[19] and was used as a store until it was demolished in 1903.[20] St Thomas Bermondsey is another prominent church with a fascinating history of alternative use, both before and after its closure in 1898. It had already, during a period of dilapidation, served as the home of an operating theatre to St Thomas' hospital in the 18th century, and was to become the chapter house for the cathedral following the creation of Southwark Diocese in 1905.[21] Whatever the background it is striking that when the Phillimore Report recommended the demolition

Figure 6 St Matthew, Spring Gardens, London, used as a store, shortly before its demolition in 1903. Image from *Survey of London: Volume 20*, courtesy of British History Online, http://www.british-history.ac.uk/survey-london/vol20/pt3/plate-39

of a further 19 City of London churches in 1919, a report of the London County Council responded with the suggestion that it would be worth retaining the church buildings even if their furnishing were removed, in other words if put to alternative use.[22]

The argument for alternative use of closed churches instead of demolition was growing, but the ability of the institutional Church of England to get legislation through parliament was weaker than it had been for some time, given the pressure on the parliamentary timetable. It was this that led to a proposal that the Church should have the power to make its own 'measures', which would be debated in a Church Assembly and then laid before Parliament for approval. The Church of England Assembly (Powers) Act 1919, also known as the Enabling Act, was designed for this purpose. Its passing led to the ability of the Established Church to set out its own policy on church closure in the Union of Benefices Measure 1923, a measure which allowed, as mentioned above, for the alternative use of closed churches for educational, charitable or other purposes related to the Church of England.

But what provided for the further leap towards wider alternative use was the destruction caused by the Second World War. The idea that churches could be put to a wider range of uses than those in the Union of Benefice Measure 1923 was contained in the provisions of the Reorganisation of Areas Measures 1944 to 1954, which were adopted to deal with the problem of churches in heavily war-damaged areas. The issue of bomb damage also required attention in the City of London. Resistance to city church closure had become strong from the 1880s, and the rate of church closures in the city had slowed rapidly after the initial closures under the 1860 Act in the late 1860s and 1870s. But the bombing of so many city churches required attention, and a report of 1944 entitled 'The City Churches: Interim Report of the Bishop of London's Commission' was published under the chairpersonship of former solicitor general, Lord Merriman. The Commission was established in 1941 and its final report, after 20 meetings, was published in January 1946. Part of the report was to welcome the notion that some of the war-damaged sites could be utilized to build social institutes, and that three churches – St Stephen, Coleman Street; Christ Church, Greyfriars; and St Dunstan in the East – could be converted to church halls and used for young people as extra parochial buildings. Likewise it was suggested St Augustine, Watling Street be put to use by St Paul's Cathedral as a chapter house or choir school.[23]

The concept of wider alternative use was later applied to the last revision of the Union of Benefices Measure in 1952. When Second Church Estates Commissioner Sir John Crowder (1890–1961) asked Parliament to approve the Measure, he did so saying:

> The Committee recommended that the power given under the Union of Benefices Measure should be extended so as to make the wider powers of the Reorganisation of Areas Measure of general permanent application. The general object of this Measure is to give effect to that recommendation. A particular effect would be to authorise redundant churches to be put to such wider use – as an example, for use as a museum or perhaps for use by the Boy Scouts. This will relieve parochial authorities in relevant cases from the burden of upkeep of the buildings which are no longer required for religious worship and which might otherwise fall into disrepair and generally in time into ruin. This Measure will, of course, help the Historic Churches Preservation Trust in its object of preserving historic churches. Under this Measure the Church Commissioners may prepare and submit to Her Majesty in Council a scheme to give effect to proposals made by the pastoral committee, with the bishop's consent, for demolishing a redundant church and the sale of the materials on the site, excluding any land which is used as a churchyard, and may appropriate the church or any part of it to such use as may be specified in the scheme.[24]

But even then there were objections. Godfrey Nicholson (1901–1991), Conservative MP for Farnham, expressed his anxieties about the openness of the provisions on alternative use, stating, 'There is nothing in the Measure to prevent a church becoming a cinema. I know it is ridiculous to suggest that a bishop would permit that, but, technically, there is nothing in the Measure to prevent that.' He even suggested that St Paul's Cathedral could be tuned into a cinema under the provisions of the Measure.[25] The answer to his anxieties was that such a use would have to be agreed as part of a closure scheme, and it was is clear from the debate that use of a former church as a cinema was regarded as inappropriate.

Interestingly some of the most iconic examples of alternative use are churches bombed during the war but for which an alternative use was not found for several years. These include St John's Smith Square, bombed in 1941 and a ruin for over 20 years until it was restored as a concert venue in the 1960s. It now advertises it services as, among other things, 'a film and video location'.[26]

A key personality in the discussions around church closure in the post-war period was Percy Herbert (1885–1968), bishop of Norwich from 1942 to 1959. Indeed, perhaps because of the Norwich context, bishops of the diocese have tended to be prominent in

Figure 7 St John, Smith Square, London, now used as a concert venue and film location. Photo by Steve Cadman from London, U.K. (St John) [CC BY-SA 2.0 (http://creativecommons.org/licenses/by-sa/2.0)], via Wikimedia Commons

national church closure discussion. Herbert chaired a committee that reported to the Church Assembly in 1948 with suggestions that certain churches of historic interest and/or architectural merit no longer required for public worship should be placed in the care of the Ministry of Works. The idea was supported, and a list of 111 possible candidates for guardianship was put together, but this led to no further action on the part of the government during a period of 'national financial stringency'.[27] Rather it was left for the Church to seek further solutions to what was becoming known as 'the problem of redundant churches', hence the establishment of an Archbishops' Commission which sat from 1958 to 1960 with former senior civil servant Lord Edward Bridges (1892–1969) as chair. The report of the commission sought to clarify and simplify the law related to church closure, which was then governed by three distinct procedures: the 1860 Act, the Union of Benefices Measures 1923–1952, and the Reorganisation of Areas Measures 1944–1954. The commission took evidence on a range of issues, including alternative use, and it made proposals which were eventually to form the basis of the closure procedures contained in the Pastoral Measure 1968.

On alternative use, it reported that its evidence-taking had revealed:

There was general agreement among witnesses that more positive efforts should be made to find suitable alternative use. The Georgian Group suggested the setting up of an Historic Churches Bureau on the lines of the Historic Buildings Bureau of the Ministry of Works. All secular bodies who expressed views on the matter favoured the transfer where practicable to any other Christian denomination. Other uses suggested as suitable were as a library, museum, concert or lecture hall. Commercial or industrial uses would be unseemly in a building which had been a church and continued to look like one, and partly because physical injury to the building itself would be more likely to result from the works of alteration.[28]

Thus it was that among its various recommendations the Commission suggested the establishment of what became the Redundant Churches Fund (later the Churches Conservation Trust, CCT) as the main organization for the preservation of churches, but also recommendations such as the establishment of a Uses Committee of the Church Commissioners to advise dioceses on appropriate future uses, and the proposal to allow wider alternative use, including by other Christian denominations and for secular purposes.[29]

During the sitting of the commission, Bishop Herbert cannot have been unaware of the challenges presented by the number of historic churches in his own diocese, and not least in his cathedral city. The Bridges Report included a photograph of St Peter Hungate, which was already being used as a museum of ecclesiastical art from 1936. The use as a museum was clearly under a liberal interpretation of the Union of Benefice Measure, that a church could be 'appropriated for educational, charitable or other purposes in connection with the Church of England having in view the spiritual, intellectual, moral or social welfare of the Parishioners of the United Parish and others'.[30]

According to the Friends of Norwich Museums, St Peter Hungate 'became the first Anglican Church to be turned into secular use'.[31] The Friends, originally founded in 1920 as the Friends of the Castle Museum, was one of a number of local societies in Norwich which helped to preserve the city's built heritage. The Norwich Society had earlier prevented the demolition of St Simon and St Jude,[32] and it was the Norfolk Archaeological Trust which helped save St Peter from demolition.[33]

It was left to Herbert's successor, Launcelot Fleming (1906–1990), bishop of Norwich from 1959 to 1971, to grapple with the wider problem of the Norwich city churches. Fleming established his own commission, chaired by former Conservative government minister Lord Brooke (1903–1984). This proposed the retention of only six city centre churches for parish use, and that the rest be subject to the new procedures for redundancy adopted under the Pastoral Measure. On alternative use it entertained the suggestion that a 'Friends of the Norwich City Churches' be formed – as then happened with the formation of the Norwich Historic Churches Trust (NCHT) – and suggested various uses to which churches made redundant could be put, including many of the uses which such churches were indeed to be put in the years thereafter. Interestingly it expressed a more positive view of commercial use than the Bridges report, stating:

> As to commercial uses, it is the Commission's view that a commercial use which would ensure the careful upkeep of the building and enable the beauty of the interior to continue to be seen may be more acceptable than a social use of a kind which would

Figure 8 A pioneering reuse: St Peter Hungate, Norwich as a museum. Photo by George Plunkett, 1938, reproduced by kind permission of Jonathan Plunkett.

unhappily blot out those aesthetic qualities that may justify the building's retention.[34]

On one level there is no better place to observe how alternative use has developed since 1969 than Norwich, where 31 medieval churches populate the city in addition to the cathedral, the rebuilt medieval church of St Julian, and several church buildings belonging to non-Anglicans. Eight of the 31 remain in the care of the Church of England and are used for regular public worship, three are vested with the CCT, one is maintained as a ruin, one is in private ownership, and the other 18 are looked after by the NHCT. Since most of these churches were put into the care of the NHCT in the 1970s, and others acquired since, alternative use has included a centre of hospitality, a pregnancy crisis centre, artists' studios, a puppet theatre, an Orthodox church, a community church, exhibition spaces, business spaces, a base for the Scouts, a brass-rubbing centre, a bookshop, and homes for the Norwich Night Shelter, the Association for the Care and Resettlement of Offenders, the Norwich Arts Centre, the Inspire Discovery Centre museum, the Anglian Academy of Dance, and the Norwich Academy of Martial Arts. Alternative use of churches, and indeed of other kinds of building, has become part of the social fabric of Norwich, and the NHCT has become expert in managing the challenges and opportunities that alternative use affords.

However, there are several reasons why Norwich is not a good example of what alternative use looks like throughout the rest of the England, even if only compared with other urban centres. This is not just because the number of redundant churches in Norwich, 23, is more than anywhere else in England, but because the extent of social and community use in Norwich is proportionally greater than elsewhere in the country. Of other urban centres with high listings on the Church of England's Closed Churches Statistics Database,[35] Bristol has the next highest number of city-centre closure schemes. There, 16 schemes led to one site disposal, one demolition, one part-demolition, one residential use, one use as an Orthodox church, one technical closure to allow for external funding, and seven community-type uses (including a concert hall, climbing centre and sports centre). Only three Bristol churches are vested in the CCT, and one of those, St Paul, is now used as a circus school.[36] It makes a difference, of course, that only three of these 16 were medieval churches. The rest were constructed in the 18th and 19th centuries, and only four of these have a Grade 2* or Grade 1 listing.

York is more like Norwich. With eight closure schemes there were one demolition, two vestings with the CCT, and five conversions to community use (including museums, a place of refreshment, and an elderly persons' day centre). More typical of urban church closure are places like Blackburn (where eight schemes have led to two site clearances, four demolitions, one vesting and one community use), Preston (where eight schemes have led to one use by another denomination, one as a studio, one conversion to residential flats, one as a hostel, one demolition, one part-demolition, one museum and one technical closure), and Birkenhead (where nine schemes have led to one part-community/part-church use, one museum, two site disposals and five demolitions). Only Ipswich operates like Norwich, with a Historic Churches Trust as guardian of several churches, and there it cares for only five churches, all as community-use-type spaces.[37]

Taking figures on redundancy from 1969 to 2002,[38] 21 per cent of redundant churches were earmarked for preservation, whereas in Norwich this figure is 13 per cent; 22 per cent of redundant churches were demolished, whereas none were demolished in this period in Norwich; and 57 per cent were designated for alternative use, whereas in Norwich this figure is 80 per cent. What is more, whereas the range of alternative uses nationwide included 13 per cent residential use and 0.8 per cent sports use, with only 14 per cent put to civic or cultural purposes, for Norwich none were converted to residential or sports use and the vast majority are used for civic or cultural purposes. So, as great as an example as Norwich may be of best practice on alternative use, it is not typical of the general picture of alternative use across England.

A more typical example of urban alternative use can be found with a consideration of church closure in the diocese of Liverpool, with the examples below giving a stronger sense of some of the controversy related to the use, reuse and abuse of alternative use.

St Ann, Warrington[39] is a case in point. From 1993 onwards the vicar, the Reverend Steve Parish, actively campaigned for the church's closure. He agreed with the diocese that the church was isolated in an area mostly used for industry, that the building was in need of repair, that it was expensive to maintain and that a new church building was needed to serve the needs of the congregation. However, Steve Parish felt that the bishop was not doing enough to market the site, and so wrote an article in *Church Building* suggesting that the building was ideal for adaption to offices, and calling for 'an architect on a white horse … looking for a new headquarters'.[40] This is the only example among the Liverpool church closure case files held by the Church Commissioners where a party provided formal theological justification for the closure of a church. This was expressed

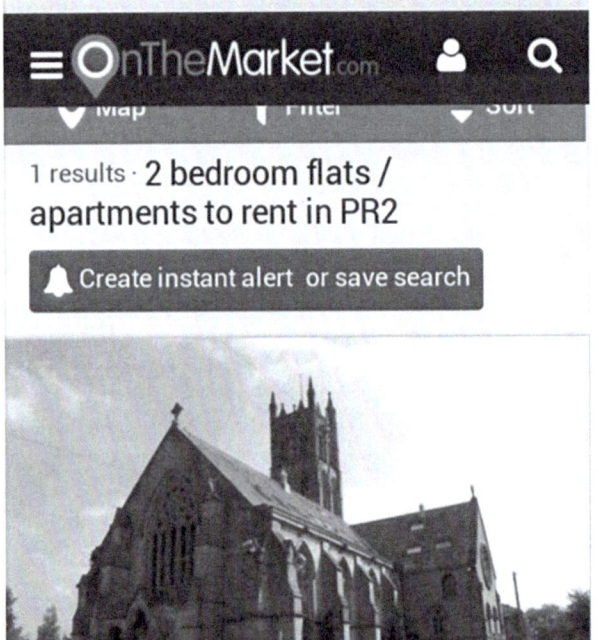

Figure 9 St Mark, Preston: converted into residential accommodation (from the agent's website).

in a report commissioned by the archdeacon of Warrington. The report was written by a Church of England reader, who was also a student of Victorian architecture and a member of the Victorian Society. The report, completed in 1993, included the comment:

> The primary purpose of the church is to serve people and not to preserve buildings. We have no abiding city here. It is the theology of the tabernacle that is applicable to church buildings, rather than that of the temple. Christians are a pilgrim people.

This was certainly not the official line of the Victorian Society itself, which did not oppose closure or alternative use as such, but did oppose the demolition of St Ann, citing the loss of other churches in Warrington. It also opposed the internal alteration to the church represented by the emerging proposal that the building become a climbing centre, a proposal eventually confirmed in a scheme of 1995. For the local media, the new use gave rise to such headlines as 'Heaven's Above – new flock will scale the walls.'[41]

Other alternative uses proposed for closed churches also caused occasional controversy in the diocese. For example, the *Warrington Guardian* reported 'howls of protest' at the proposal for the closure of St Peter, Warrington, which Thwaites Brewery proposed mostly to demolish, but with the retention of some of the walls for a public house on the site.[42] Yet

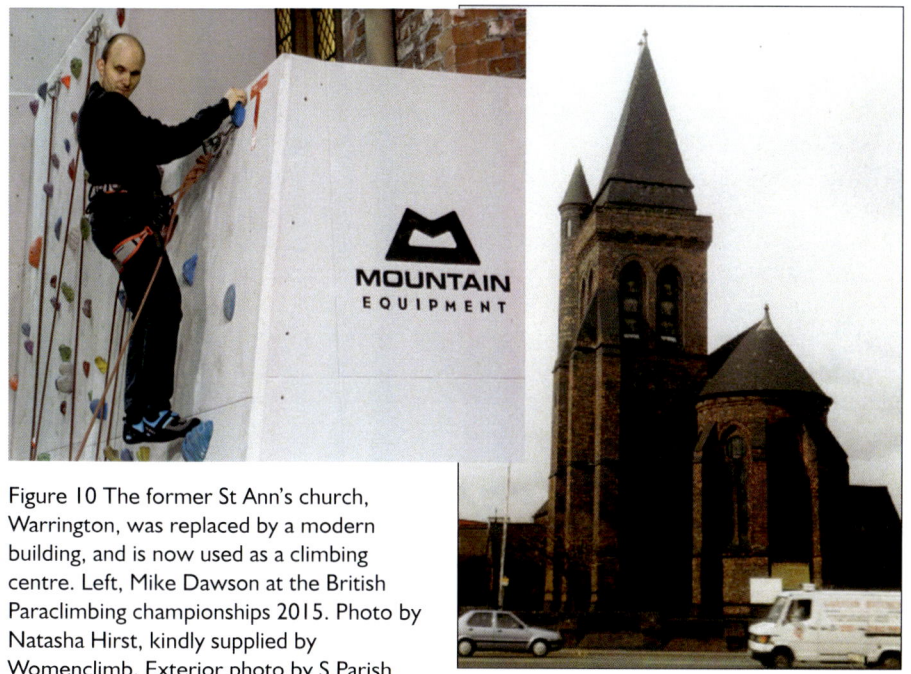

Figure 10 The former St Ann's church, Warrington, was replaced by a modern building, and is now used as a climbing centre. Left, Mike Dawson at the British Paraclimbing championships 2015. Photo by Natasha Hirst, kindly supplied by Womenclimb. Exterior photo by S Parish [CC BY-SA 2.0 (http://creativecommons.org/licenses/by-sa/2.0)], via Wikimedia Commons.

unlike objections a hundred years before, the reasons given were to do with anxiety about noise levels rather than feelings that it would be inappropriate to put a pub on the site of a former church.

Noise, then, proved more controversial than alcohol, but neither noise nor alcohol, nor gambling nor politics, caused controversy at St Cuthbert, Everton. When the church closed as part of a scheme to unite its parish with neighbouring St Saviour, Everton, the diocese started the use-seeking process. The first possibility to emerge, in 1970, was conversion to a sweet and tobacco factory. There was little enthusiasm for this from the diocese or the Commissioners. Then a new proposal emerged, namely purchase by the Conservative and Unionist Party to take on the church as a headquarters and a club. The diocesan secretary, in suggesting this idea to the Commissioners, enquired:

> When it doth come to pass that the sale of this church becomes a probability would you please confirm that the Commissioners have no objection to the premises being acquired by a political organisation for use as a headquarters and social club in which alcohol will be consumed and tobacco smoked. It may also be possible that a sweepstake might be held from time to time.[43]

The bishop's views were sought on the proposal, and he is reported to have thought it a good idea. The Church Commissioner's officer dealing with the file added a note saying, 'The area is solidly Protestant, which in Liverpool is apparently equivalent to being supporters of the Conservative and Unionist Party. The use of the church by the local branch of the Party would therefore be acceptable to local residents.' But in the end it did not come to pass, not because of opposition to the proposal but because the church was badly vandalized. It became unsafe and was demolished in 1972.

Another proposal involving politics did prove controversial. This was the proposal drafted in 1974 that St Polycarp, Everton be leased to the Protestant Reformers Memorial Church (PMRC). The Reverend Roger Sainsbury, vicar of nearby St Ambrose and St Timothy, and a Reverend N. J. Patterson, a nearby curate, both objected, claiming the church had links with the Orange Order and that 'their identification with the extreme Protestant group in Northern Ireland' would 'rekindle old enmities' between Protestants and Roman Catholics in Liverpool. The bishop, however, had no objections and received assurances that the PMRC was not linked to paramilitary activity and condemned violence. The church was sold to the PMRC in 1975. It used the building for a number of years, but then gave it up, and the diocese found a new use for it as an arts studio in 2000.[44]

This was not the only case in the diocese where controversial use by another faith organization was put to the test. In 1975, there was a suggestion that St Mark, Edge Lane be used by the Fourth Church of Christ Scientist. The Church Commissioners' advice was that the proposal would not be dismissed out of hand, but that since the church had no relations with the British Council of Churches it would be a policy matter whether use would be suitable in accordance with Section 51 (1) (a) of the Pastoral Measure.[45] The phrase 'policy matter' really meant that it would be a matter of specific decision for the Commissioners whether or not to allow use by a sect or other faith organization, a decision that the Commissioners were, and still are, reluctant to make. Only two closed churches are currently used by another faith, both as Sikh temples.

There was also an example in Liverpool diocese of the use by another Christian organization proving controversial after the use was agreed. Christ Church Kensington was closed in 1977 and used for storage purposes before being sold on to Deya Ministries in 2002. In 2006, the BBC covered the arrest for child trafficking of Kenyan Evangelist Bishop Gilbert Deya of Deya Ministries. He claimed to have created miracle babies through the power of prayer. There is no indication that the Commissioners sought to take any action in relation to the building.[46]

This is an interesting contrast to the case of St Nathaniel, Edge Hill, where the church, sold in 1982 and used for the manufacture of garden sheds, attracted the attention of the Commissioners in 1990. The Diocesan Registrar asked the Commissioners to write to the owners pointing out that they had breached the covenants on use of the building by showing a play. It further disturbed the Registrar that the play included 'masturbation, boys kissing, abortion and suicide'. As it happened, no more plays were shown in the church and the manufacture of sheds came to an end. This led to the eventual demolition of the church in 1993, following a request from the City Council to use the land for urban regeneration.[47]

One more example from Liverpool is worth considering in order to highlight issues related to the reuse of closed churches. St James, Toxteth[48] has a complex history, not least because after years of indecision about its future, it is now back in use as a parish church. It was built in 1774 and became the subject of redundancy discussions in 1970, around the use of the site for the Liverpool Inner Ring Motorway under powers related

Figure 11 Now a Sikh temple: St Luke Newton, Southampton. Photo kindly supplied by Singh Sabha Gurdwara, Southampton.

to the Liverpool Corporation Act 1966. The Advisory Board of the Council for the Care of Churches was consulted and refused to agree with proposals for demolition in 1971, since St James was the only surviving 18th-century Anglican church in Liverpool, and the only known surviving church by the architect Cuthbert Bisbrowne. A post-1985 Advisory Board report indicated that various potential new uses had been considered, including by a community-based landscaping project (the 'Diggers'); by the Church of Gospel Ministry; by MENCAP, as a nursing home; by a firm of organ builders; as a holistic health centre; as an art/crafts complex; and as a studio of Liverpool Polytechnic.

However, since all of these proposals came to nothing, a scheme was drafted in 1976 to vest the building in the Redundant Churches Fund. The scheme was opposed by the Reverend Jack Webb of West Wickham. He argued that 'it would not be right to preserve this church as an empty building in the heart of Liverpool', and that he wished that the church be put to some more useful function or demolished. What is particularly fascinating here is the response of the then bishop of Liverpool, David Shepherd. He argued that the church might be needed again, saying that 'there were large scale housing developments in the area'. The Board recommended vesting, but there was much discussion on whether 'mothballing' with the Redundant Churches Fund was an appropriate use of its resources. (This would have meant just leaving the church with an extended waiting period beyond the three-year maximum during which, under the legislation, a church for which no future is identified should be demolished.) Members of the Board expressed different views, including the view that this was precisely one of the uses of the Fund, 'to care for a church with the possibility that it might one day return to parish use'.

Once the Redundant Churches Fund had become the Churches Conservation Trust, it considered several potential uses for the church as an alternative to continued vesting. Among these were use by a pentecostal church, as a nursing home, as an organ builder's workshop, as a health centre, as an arts and crafts complex, by a local Ghanaian group, by a credit union, and as a media centre for Edge Hill University. Solid interest was shown by Potters House Fellowship in 2005, but the organization then pulled out. Next the CCT

Figure 12 Restored to parish use: St James in the City, Liverpool. Photo by the author, 2016.

Figure 13 Not the done thing in England: the Triple Kirks pub in Aberdeen. Photo by the author, 2016.

considered leasing St James as an interfaith community centre. Again, the plan came to nothing. Then in August 2009 the bishop of Liverpool, James Jones, was instrumental in creating a pastoral scheme to make a new parish, St James in the City, and bring the closed church back into use as the parish church. This was only the second time this had happened in the Church of England. The previous example of a church being 'de-vested' was St Lawrence, Didmarton (in the diocese of Gloucester) in 1991, but it has happened with a number of other churches since the reopening of St James in the City.

Although 'alternative use' is a different closure category from 'preservation', the example above indicates that these categories are not rigid. A closed church can pass from one kind of use to another, and even reopen as a parish church. The strain on resources in recent years has led the CCT in the direction of regarding regeneration as a resource for preservation, with the aforementioned Bristol circus school a prime example of this approach. Likewise, heritage enthusiasts have long accepted that sometimes conversion of a closed church to another use is the best means of ensuring the preservation of the building. In the 1970s an exhibition at the Victoria & Albert Museum, *Change and Decay,* highlighted issues to do with church closure, and the publication that followed in 1976 included a chapter recommending 'New uses for churches'.[49]

The campaigning organization SAVE endorsed this approach in its 1987 publication *Churches: A Question of Conversion.*[50] Several other publications on closed churches also commended the approach,[51] including documents by English Heritage.[52] SAVE's 2011 publication *London's Churches are Fighting Back,*[53] which revisited churches about which it expressed concern in its 1985 report *London's Churches are Falling Down,*[54] was more positive about some of the churches converted to commercial use, such as Christ Church, Cosway Street and St Mark, North Audley Street, than it was about churches such as St Columbia, Kingsland Road, used by Christ Apostolic Church since its redundancy scheme in 1974, but in a very dilapidated state.

SAVE is not alone in questioning whether the solutions for dealing with closure in the past were the right solutions for the longer-term future of many churches. Richard Chartres, bishop of London since 1995, has been a strong voice against church closure, and has supported the reopening of closed churches, such as St Luke, Oseney Crescent, reopened as a parish church in 2011 after many years in the care of the CCT. Chartres has also supported the creative use of churches in the City of London, resisting the closure recommendations of the 1994 Templeman Report[55] which he inherited upon his enthronement. Instead he assisted with church reopening via the work of the Friends of the City Churches[56] and others.

At the same time Bishop Chartres, for many years the Church of England's lead bishop for cathedrals and church buildings, has championed investment in living churches to prevent closure, and the view that alternative use is possible even within a living parish church. Indeed this was one of the few changes permitted in the revision of the most recent revision of the regulations concerning church closure. The Mission and Pastoral Measure 2011 allowed for the part-licensing of a church for purposes other than worship, as has happened, for example, at St Aubyn, Devonport. This Grade 2 listed Georgian building now serves as the town library, but services still take place on a mezzanine floor in front of the stained-glass window in the east end.[57]

Before concluding, it is worth noting the contrast between alternative use of Church

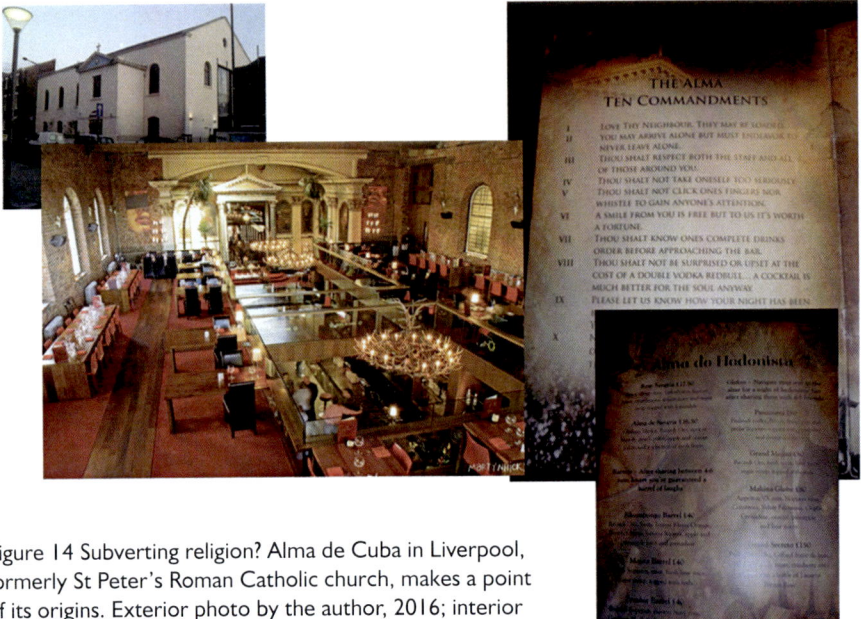

Figure 14 Subverting religion? Alma de Cuba in Liverpool, formerly St Peter's Roman Catholic church, makes a point of its origins. Exterior photo by the author, 2016; interior photo from www.alma-de-cuba.com

of England churches and use of closed churches by other denominations. Scottish cities, for their own historical reasons, contain many church buildings which have been put to a whole manner of uses which would not meet with the approval of the Church Commissioners, not least as establishments for the consumption of alcohol. There are exceptions, including the Brick Lane Music Theatre in the closed church of St Mark, Silvertown, where alcohol can certainly be purchased at the bar. But the use of former Anglican churches as pubs and clubs, in the manner of Liverpool's Alma de Cuba, formerly St Peter's Roman Catholic Church, is certainly the exception to the rule. The *Telegraph* report of a 'church used as a nightclub' was related to the Anglican church of Holy Trinity, Kingsway, but as the article made clear, such use was not authorized, but in the Archdeacon's words, 'done without our permission'.[58] The press are not always clear about denomination in their reporting, but the discerning scholar of Anglican church closure can easily spot that neither Bed City in Leicester nor a Tesco in Bournemouth is located in a former Church of England building.

In summary, alternative use of Church of England closed churches generally falls somewhere between the popularized images of nightclubs and bed stores, and the more sober community uses found in Norwich. The history of alternative use reveals that it was not always regarded as acceptable, arose with opposition, and proceeded with controversy. It raises questions about why alternative use became acceptable, and more research is needed on how attitudes began to change, particularly at the beginning of the 20th century. That a shift took place is undeniable: a shift from paramount concern about preserving the significance of what took place inside the building, namely divine worship, to preserving the significance of what was represented by the outside of the building. It is too simple to suggest that this was just the working-out of secularization, for on one

Figure 15 St Peter Parmentergate, Norwich, now a martial arts centre. Photo by the author.

level preserving church buildings, regardless of their internal use, was a form of preserving religiosity in the urban landscape.

That it mattered for the Church of England, far more than for other denominations, what took place inside former church buildings, and that attitudes changed in relation to this only gradually, is perhaps evidence of how the established Church sought to preserve something of its special relationship with the state, even with buildings no longer needed for public worship. Moreover, that the Church of England held, for a long time, such a strict either/or attitude to 'worship' or 'secular use' is perhaps an indication of how far the Anglican church was itself affected by the secularizing mind-set of regarding religion as a separate sphere of human activity from the rest of life.

As understandings continue to develop about the future of church closure, it cannot be taken for granted that alternative use will continue to remain helpful as a rigid category of future use, or that understandings of what it permits will remain the same. As dual use of church buildings becomes more common again, as it was in the pre-modern period, it is even possible that 'alternative use' of closed churches might itself become redundant.

Steven Saxby is a PhD student at Kings College London.

Appendix 1: The destination of redundant church buildings, 1969–2002

	Number	Per cent
Alternative use (details below)	**925**	**57**
Civic cultural or community purposes	229	14
Residential use	204	13
Monuments	137	8
Worship by other Christian bodies	119	7
Light industrial/office/shopping	57	4
Arts and crafts, music or drama centres	36	2
Storage	35	2
Private school chapels	25	2
Educational purposes	24	1.5
Museums	16	1.0
Adjuncts to adjoining estates	10	0.6
Sports use	13	0.8
Masonic halls	3	0.2
Worship by non-Christian faith	2	0.1
Restored to parish use/chapel of ease	15	0.9
Demolition and site disposal	**360**	**22**
To housing associations	69	4
To local authorities	48	3
For other community purposes	23	1.4
For new places of worship	60	4
As additions to churchyards	46	3
To other purchasers	111	7
Undecided	3	0.2
Preservation	**341**	**21**
By Churches Conservation Trust	331	20
By Diocesan Boards of Finance	6	0.4
By Department of the Environment	4	0.2
Total	**1,626**	**100**

Source: Church Commissioners Redundant Churches Committee, Report, 2002

Appendix 2: Key legislation

Union of Benefices Act 1860
Union of Benefices Measures 1923–1952
Reorganisation of Areas Measures 1944–1954
Pastoral Measure 1968, then 1983
Mission and Pastoral Measure 2011

Notes

1. Unless a church, by virtue of its historical significance or architectural quality, is preserved by vesting in the care of the Churches Conservation Trust (CCT) or some other body, an alternative use for the church is sought. Only if no alternative use can be found, and vesting is not considered appropriate, will the church authorities pursue the third option of demolishing the church. The provisions were first contained in the Pastoral Measure 1968 and the Redundant Churches and Other Religious Buildings Act 1969, and most recently in the Mission and Pastoral Measure 2011.
2. Linda Monkton, *Churches and Closure in the Church of England: A Summary Report* (London: English Heritage,2010).
3. Nicholas Groves, *The Medieval Churches of the City of Norwich* (Norwich, 2010).
4. 37 Hen. VIII c.20, Benefices Act 1545.
5. D. M. Palliser, 'The unions of parishes at York, 1547-1586', *Yorkshire Archaeological Journal* 46 (1974), 94.
6. See Neil Batcock, 'The ruined and disused churches of Norfolk', *East Anglia Archaeology* (1993).
7. www.bradwellchapel.org/chapel.html (accessed 15 October 2015).
8. Gordon L. Barnes, *London's Redundant Churches* (London: Ecclesiological Society, 1972), p. 6.
9. Gerald Cobb, *London's City Churches* (London, 1977), pp. 123–5.
10. Richard Lambert Jones, *Reminiscences of the Public Life of R. L. J.* (London, 1863), pp. 45–47.
11. Lambert Jones, *Reminiscences of the Public Life of R. L. J.*, pp. 45–7.
12. Additionally for use as school rooms. Parliamentary Papers, 23 & 24 Vict. 10 July 1860, A Bill as amended in committee intitled An Act to make better Provision for the Union of contiguous Benefices in Cities, Towns and Boroughs, Clause, 18.
13. Hansard, HL Deb 26 April 1860 vol. 158 c121. 'Socianism' was derived from the non-Trinitarian theology of Italian-born Faustus Socinus (1539–1604), whose thoughts were adopted by the Polish Brethren. In the 19th century it was a catch-all term for any kind of dissenting religion.
14. Hansard, HL Deb 15 June 1860 vol 159 c506.
15. Hansard, HC Deb 25 April 1865 vol 178 c1023.
16. HL Deb. 23 March 1886 vol 303 cc1601-05.
17. www.forgottenbooks.com/readbook_text/Report_of_the_Proceedings_1894_1000659170/617 (accessed 23 October 2015).
18. Liverpool and Wigan Churches Act 1904; Manchester Churches Act 1906.
19. Public Offices Site Act, 46/46 Vict, 32.
20. J. McMaster, *A Short History of the Royal Parish of St Martin-in-the-Fields, London* (London, 1916). A newspaper cutting in the Westminster City Archives contains a photograph of the chapel and refers to it as 'The Old Chapel Royal in Spring Gardens: now used as a store by Office of Works'.
21. It is now the 'Herb garret and operating theatre museum', www.southwark.anglican.org/downloads/lostchurches/BER13.pdf
22. *Proposed Demolition of Nineteen Churches: A report by the Clerk of the Council and the Architect of the Council* (London County Council, 1920), p. 30.
23. Also, 11 churches seriously damaged were recommended for restoration. This left five: St Mildred, Bread Street; St Mary Aldermanbury; St Alban, Wood Street; St Swithun, London Stone; and St Andrew by the Wardrobe. All but the last were not rebuilt.
24. HC Deb 04 December 1952 vol 508 cc1893–94.
25. HC Deb 04 December 1952 vol 508 cc1899
26. www.sjss.org.uk/hire-hall, accessed 19/10/15

27 *Report of the Archbishops' Commission on Redundant Churches 1958–60*, p. 20.
28 *Report of the Archbishops' Commission*, p. 34.
29 *Report of the Archbishops' Commission*, pp. 46–7.
30 The scheme for St Peter appeared in the *London Gazette* on 26 May 1933, p. 35.
31 www.friendsofthenorwichmuseums.co.uk/history.html (accessed 23 October 2015).
32 Groves, *The Medieval Churches of the City of Norwich*, p. 126.
33 Groves, *The Medieval Churches of the City of Norwich*, p. 110.
34 Diocese of Norwich, Norwich City Commission Report, pp. 23–4.
35 Closed Churches Statistics Database, accessed 20 October 2015.
36 www.visitchurches.org.uk/Ourchurches/Completelistofchurches/St-Pauls-Church-Bristol-Bristol/, accessed 20/10/15.
37 www.ipswichhistoricchurchestrust.org.uk/, accessed 20 October 2015.
38 Published in Trevor Cooper, 'How do keep our parish churches?' (2004), p. 64.
39 Church Commissioners, RC22/193.
40 *Church Building*, Winter/Spring 1993.
41 *Warrington Guardian*, 24 November 1995.
42 *Warrington Guardian*, 3 April 1981.
43 Church Commissioners, RC22/56b.
44 Church Commissioners, RC22/55.
45 Church Commissioners, RC22/112.
46 BBC News, 14 February 2006.
47 Church Commissioners, RC22/41b.
48 Church Commissioner, RC22/180.
49 Patrick Brown, 'New uses for churches', pp. 163–70 in Marcus Binney and Peter Burman, *Change and Decay: The Future of Our Churches* (London, 1976).
50 Ken Powell and Celia de la Hay, *Churches – a Question of Conversion* (London, 1987).
51 John G. Davies, *The Secular Use of Church Buildings* (London, 1969); Derek Latham, *Creative Re-use of Buildings, Vols 1 and 2* (Shaftesbury: Donhead, 2000); Sherbon Cantacuzino, *Re-Architecture: Old Buildings/New Uses* (New York, 1989); Christopher John Kiley, *Convert! The Adaptive Reuse of Churches* (MCP and SM thesis in real estate development, Dept. of Urban Studies and Planning, Massachusetts Institute of Technology, 2004).
52 English Heritage, 'New uses for former places of worship' (2010, updated 2012).
53 SAVE, *London's Churches are Fighting Back* (London, 2011).
54 SAVE, *London's Churches are Falling Down* (London, 1985).
55 Diocese of London, City Churches Commission: The Diocese of London: Report to the Bishop of London, 1994.
56 www.london-city-churches.org.uk/ (accessed 20 October 2015).
57 *Church Times*, 25 March 2011, p. 4.
58 *Daily Telegraph*, 10 August 1987.

Working co-operatively with closed churches: the Holland Coastal Group

Stella Jackson

Introduction

In 2013 the Society for the Protection of Ancient Buildings (SPAB) launched a new three-year, HLF-funded Maintenance Co-operatives Project (MCP). This ground-breaking initiative aims to build capacity and promote best practice, by bringing together and supporting groups of volunteers to help look after local places of worship in five regions across England: the North East, Lincolnshire, Cumbria, Herefordshire and Worcestershire, and the South West. This paper focuses on one of the groups which has been set up in Lincolnshire, to the east of Boston, and mainly on one particular church in that group, All Saints, Benington.

The Maintenance Co-operatives Project

The MCP is the successor to the SPAB's HLF-backed Faith in Maintenance project, which ran for five years between 2007 and 2012, and delivered 150 maintenance training courses to around 5,000 volunteers. This follow-on project has been running since the autumn of 2013 and has one important aim: to connect, encourage and support people who care for their local places of worship, with more than just a training course.

We are doing this by:

- creating a series of locally based networks – local maintenance co-operatives – to share good maintenance practice and help the people responsible for places of worship to take good care of their buildings
- training churchwardens, fabric officers, property stewards and other volunteers responsible for, or interested in the care of places of worship, so that they can confidently look after day-to-day maintenance issues themselves
- supporting the recruitment of new volunteers to help look after places of worship
- sharing good maintenance practice with the wider community.

A maintenance co-operative is a group of volunteers who support each other in the regular preventive maintenance of a group of local places of worship, and is formed as an unincorporated organization when places of worship and/or volunteers agree to form it. Usually it begins with a core group of church wardens and fabric officers. Membership of a group is gradually increased to include not just other churches, however, but new people from the local area, especially those who might not be members of the congregation, but who are very interested in looking after the building.

Each co-op group is essentially a network of people to call on, for example, to see if members can recommend a good local roofer, or have equipment that they might lend to other churches rather than each one buying it separately. Members also meet up at training events and working parties, which include opportunities to share knowledge and ideas over a cup of tea. There is a strong social, community aspect to the groups, therefore. It is all about working together co-operatively, as the name suggests.

The co-operative is supported and encouraged by the SPAB to carry out a programme of planned preventive maintenance at the places of worship in the group, which is intended to stop decay before it starts. Preventive maintenance is a set of simple but effective tasks which are carried out throughout the year to help prevent big expensive problems in the future. This might include walking round the building with a pair of binoculars to spot problems such as slipped tiles, blocked drains and damp patches; tackling overgrown plants, or learning how to protect water pipes from frost. These annual activities can also be tailored to complement quinquennial inspection (QI) reports. Church wardens already do a lot of this work, but being involved in a co-op group provides them with the tools and the confidence to be able to undertake preventive maintenance more confidently. Doing this as part of a co-op also means having people who are doing the same thing to talk it over with, as well as swapping or sharing skills and knowledge during working parties or at training events.

A tailored training programme is also developed for each group, so if members think they need training on anything in particular, the relevant project officer can organize something on it, or put them in touch with people who can help. All groups, however, are trained on how to undertake a baseline condition survey of the places of worship that they look after, after which they survey all buildings within the group and work towards preparing maintenance schedules/plans. They will also resurvey the buildings on an annual basis, providing a long-term record of the condition of the building which complements the more detailed five yearly QI report.

The Holland Coastal Co-operative

The Holland Coastal Maintenance Co-op is made up of a number of open churches, and one closed church which is currently undergoing a major repair and reordering project to turn it into a community hub. The co-operative covers an area to the east of Boston, and the name Holland Coastal has been given to the group as the early members were all part of a former parish group with this name. The members of this co-op prefer to undertake maintenance on their own churches themselves, rather than getting together as working parties. They do enjoy the chance to meet up and hear from other churches at meetings, training events and survey days, though, especially where someone is the only person looking after an isolated rural church.

The closed church is All Saints, Benington (Figure 1), a beautiful Grade I listed church of 13th century construction which retains many of its original features despite a 19th-century restoration (BCHT, n.d.*b*). Sadly the church has officially been closed since 2003, mainly because of the declining population, reduced church attendance and a

Figure 1 All Saints Church, Benington, Boston. ©SPAB.

mounting repair bill which had begun to exceed the ability of the remaining churchgoers to sustain (Churches Conservation Trust, n.d.). This situation is not uncommon. But neither is it permanent – the fortunes of such buildings have often ebbed and flowed over the centuries. What was different in this case was that the local community had already lost many of their other facilities (their GP, the local school, the post office, village shop and butchers) and they were not prepared to let that process continue (CCT, n.d).

Creating a community hub: the Beonna

Benington Community Heritage Trust (BCHT) was established in 2007 to find an alternative use for All Saints, Benington, and to bring the church back into the heart of the community (BCHT, n.d.*a*). The trust was formed as a registered building preservation trust from a small group of the Friends of All Saints, and in consultation with the local community, they began to work on the idea of creating a community hub called the Beonna. Being a preservation trust gave them membership to the Association of Preservation Trusts, and therefore access to a network of specialist support and advice, as well as the opportunity to share experiences with other such organizations working to save and reuse heritage buildings, in particular Heritage Lincolnshire (Churches Conservation Trust, n.d.).

In 2009, the Churches Conservation Trust (CCT), with its expertise in finding new uses for heritage buildings, was invited to form a working partnership with BCHT. The CCT was formally appointed as project manager for the Beonna in 2013, and was tasked with overseeing the development of a robust Stage 2 bid to the Heritage Lottery Fund (CCT, n.d.). As appointed project managers, the CCT worked with BCHT to ensure that a high-quality, cost-efficient design scheme for the site was produced, one which respects the building's integrity and is considerate of running costs – in particular, keeping them manageable. Its staff also worked with the trustees to develop a business model which will ensure that the site is sustainable and that a sufficient level of income is generated to support building maintenance and operational costs.

The overall aim of the Beonna is to bring rural services back to the village, including a post office and a shop. The project will also see the creation of a heritage centre and learning activities. In addition to this, the Beonna will provide volunteering and training opportunities for the local community, and will help to provide a sense of pride in an enterprising and vibrant rural village (BCHT, n.d.*a*). BCHT are already developing a number of activities and opportunities that could operate from the Beonna, including the provision of formal learning activities (workshops, talks and tours, apprenticeship programmes) which will enable the rich and varied mosaic of South Lincolnshire heritage to be explored and understood in a fun and engaging way. The Beonna will also provide people with the opportunity to undertake professional development and improve skill sets. In addition, an engaging, informative and fun interpretation package will be developed to bring to life the stories of All Saints and Benington.

At the end of September 2015, the Trust received the news that its HLF application had been successful, and it will be receiving a grant of £1.8 million to undertake the work (HLF, 2015). Being part of a co-op, which means that a number of the HLF requirements such as a maintenance schedule and community activities had already been fulfilled, certainly helped to secure this grant.

All Saints and the Maintenance Co-ops Project

When I first met members of the BCHT to discuss the MCP and how we could work together as partners, they felt that it sounded like a great idea and were keen to get involved as it aligned very well with the overall aims of the trust and of the Beonna project. Later I spent an afternoon with one of the volunteers, Shem, who took me around the church and pointed out all of the maintenance and repair problems that it faced (Figure 2). He also told me about the work that he was doing to try and tackle them, including lining old, leaky, lead gutters with PVC guttering as a short-term solution until they can afford to replace them properly.

In terms of how it fits with the Holland Coastal Co-op, All Saints has already been the venue for a number of events, including a launch day for the co-op which included sessions on maintenance and how to look after historic buildings, as well as some hands-on skills sessions such as stone masonry (see Figure 3). The then mayor of Boston, who is also a churchwarden for one of the other Holland Coastal Co-op churches, attended a maintenance drop-in day at All Saints, and gave her support to the community trust and the MCP.

The open churches in the group were happy to work with All Saints, which will be a useful base for other training and events in the future. The group were keen to point out

Figure 2 Maintenance issues at All Saints, Benington. ©SPAB.

Figure 3 Hands-on stone masonry session for volunteers. ©SPAB.

that having All Saints in the co-op will ensure that it continues to be maintained in the same way as the churches that are still part of the Diocese of Lincoln, and thus subject to faculty controls. They also felt that it would benefit from access to advice from the Diocesan Advisory Committee (DAC), which it would otherwise not have.

Training

A range of free training events at other churches have been held for the group, in which members of the trust and volunteers from Benington have taken part in. These have included:

- the open day mentioned above
- maintenance survey training at St James, Freiston (Figure 4)
- Dealing with Damp training at St Mary the Virgin, Frampton
- object care and conservation – looking after what is inside the buildings (a three-week course that was held at St Botolph in Boston)
- condition survey days at each of the churches in the co-op.

Future training events that I am organizing at the moment include:

- a winter maintenance day at St Peter and St Paul, Algarkirk, another church which has received funding from HLF for repairs and reordering, this time to create a heritage hub in partnership with the heritage skills centre in Lincoln

Figure 4 Maintenance survey training at St James, Freiston. ©SPAB.

- a 'welcoming visitors' training course which will look at interpretation, marketing, events, working with local schools and other groups, and welcoming visitors.

Summary and conclusion

When I first sent Nicholas Groves the proposal for this paper, I had hoped to be able to say that 'As this presentation has shown, by working co-operatively with those nearby, closed churches can not only be well maintained and cared for, but can continue to play a key role in their local community.' I think in time that will definitely be the case, but when I wrote that I had forgotten that things tend to take quite a while when you are working with churches, and with volunteers who have a wide range of other demands on their time. It is still early days for the Holland Coastal group, but they are all still very positive and enthusiastic. They are using the training to help them look after their buildings, and they are suggesting other topics that they would like sessions on too. Volunteers are also working together at survey days, which also include sharing ideas and equipment. I am sure that by 2016, therefore, there will be much more in terms of success that I can talk about in relation to Benington, as the Beonna project will be much more advanced by then.

Saxon Shore Co-op

Even though it is just outside my patch, I was excited to learn that HLF have agreed to the formation of a co-op in Norfolk following a request from representatives of Brancaster church who attended one of my training events in July 2015. This will be the Saxon Shore Co-op, initially being formed of the six churches in that benefice.

Stella Jackson *is Maintenance Co-operatives Project Officer: Lincolnshire for the SPAB. She is one of five regional project officers in the Maintenance Co-operatives team, and is leading on the project in Lincolnshire. Prior to joining the MCP team, Stella worked within the Designation Department at English Heritage, where she also took up a secondment as Places of Worship Advisor in the Government Advice team. In addition to her work with the SPAB, she is undertaking a PhD at the University of York looking at the contested nature of heritage and the values attached to local heritage sites.*

References

BCHT (n.d.*a*). *Benington Community Heritage Trust: Homepage* [online]. Available at: www.beningtonallsaintschurch.co.uk/Home (accessed 5 October 2015).
BCHT (n.d.*b*). *Building Futures from Buildings Past …* [online]. Available at: www.beningtonallsaintschurch.co.uk/beonna (accessed 5 October 2015).
Churches Conservation Trust (n.d.). *The Beonna at All Saints – A Thriving Heart for Village Life* [online]. Available at: www.visitchurches.org.uk/Aboutus/Regeneratingcommunities/Projectsexamplesofourregenerationwork/AthrivingheartforvillageBenington/ (accessed 5 October 2015).
Heritage Lottery Fund (2015). 'Benington Community Heritage Trust secures HLF investment' [online] www.hlf.org.uk/about-us/media-centre/press-releases/benington-community-heritage-trust-secures-hlf-investment (accessed 1 October 2015).

'With concern, but not without hope':
an overview of the
Norwich Historic Churches Trust

Nicholas Groves

The problem of redundant churches is one which affects every town with more church buildings than it needs. In many cases (Lincoln, Thetford) those declared redundant have long since vanished: the concept of 'heritage' had not been invented when they became redundant, which was usually in the later Middle Ages or the 16th century.[1] London, which had 106 parishes within the City walls, retained nearly all its medieval churches until 1666, when 86 of them were burned. Only 51 were rebuilt, already demonstrating that many were surplus to requirements.[2] The Church of England shamefully sold a significant proportion of its stock for commercial development of the sites in the later 19th century.

Norwich had (depending to some degree on how one counts) about 62 churches within the walls, ranging from some Anglo-Saxon ones which vanished so long ago that they had been forgotten until unearthed by archaeologists, to the enormous high-gothic fanes we still have. There were losses throughout the Middle Ages: Holy Trinity was replaced by the Cathedral in 1096, St John Colegate was taken over by the Blackfriars in 1226, St John Evangelist by the Greyfriars in 1300, and St Michael Conesford by the Austin Friars in 1290. St Christopher was burnt in 1286, and St Ethelbert was destroyed in the 1272 riot. These are, as it were, 'casual' losses, but there were planned losses too: St Matthew at Palace and St Margaret Newbridge were closed following depopulation of their parishes in the Black Death, and St Michael Tombland was demolished by the Normans when they moved the civic centre from Tombland.

About 20 of the remaining churches were declared redundant in the wake of the Reformation, the buildings demolished, and their sites redeveloped. This left 34 churches, all of which continued in use until 1884, when St Peter Southgate was closed and demolished; the parish was united with St Etheldreda. In 1892 SS Simon and Jude was closed and united with St George Tombland, but saved from demolition by being used as a Sunday school by St George's, though it later fell into disrepair.

A further case was that of St Mary the Less. Declared redundant in 1542 and united with St George Tombland, it was leased by the Diocese to the City, which allowed the 'Strangers' (Walloon clothworkers) to use it as a cloth hall. In 1637 they turned it into a Huguenot church, and held services in French. This continued until 1832, when it was taken over by the Swedenborgians, and in 1852 by the Catholic Apostolic Church. They died out in 1953, and the church became a parish hall, and then a furniture store. It was then sold, in about 1990, to a private owner. This model of alienation was not seen as acceptable.

A further impetus was given in 1934, when St Peter Hungate was closed: what to do with this building? Proposals included demolition and reuse of the materials to build a new suburban church, but the tide was on the turn against such treatment. Despite

Figure 1 SS Simon and Jude, looking east from the interior gallery. Photo by George Plunkett, 1938, reproduced by kind permission of Jonathan Plunkett.

misgivings in some quarters, it was turned into a museum of church art, but remained a consecrated building. It was the first redundant church in the country to be so used.

The Luftwaffe removed four in April 1942: St Benedict (of which the tower alone remains), St Paul (now under the eastern end of the flyover), St Michael at Thorn (now under a car park at the top of Thorn Lane); none of these was rebuilt. St Julian, also bombed that night, was rebuilt in 1958, owing to its connexion with Dame Julian; about half its fabric is original.

So we now have 31 surviving medieval churches in central Norwich, a higher concentration than any other town or city north of the Alps. There were later closures: St Edmund, Fishergate and St Swithin in the 1950s, and St Etheldreda in 1961. These were largely brought about by the Corporation's policy of rehousing city residents in the suburbs (especially those whose homes had been lost in the war), and so large swathes of the city gradually became depopulated. St Martin at Oak suffered a partial hit in 1942, and was repaired (it lost its tower) and turned into a parish hall. By the time the Report was published in 1973, 13 churches were already disused for worship. Of these, only five had alternative uses; the others sat empty and mouldering:[3]

St Martin at Oak (parish hall)
SS Simon and Jude (Scout HQ)
St Swithin (furniture store)
St Martin at Palace
St Clement at Fyebridge
St Lawrence
St Etheldreda.

St Peter Hungate (museum)
St Edmund Fishergate (shoe store)
St James Pockthorpe
St Saviour
St Mary Coslany
St Michael at Plea

Figure 2 St Saviour, looking east. Photo by George Plunkett, 1938, reproduced by kind permission of Jonathan Plunkett.

This meant that 18 churches were still in use, though some were on their last legs.[4]

This is the background against which the formation of the Norwich Historic Churches Trust (NHCT) is to be seen. In November 1967 Launcelot Fleming, the bishop of Norwich, set in train a major review of the city centre churches, largely triggered by the fact that settlement patterns had been moving residents from the city centre into the suburbs (a trend now being reversed). The Commission was under chairmanship of Lord Brooke of Cumnor (Henry Brooke, the controversial home secretary from 1962 to 1964), hence it is always referred to as the Brooke Report.[5] The Commission consulted widely: this included contacting all the Anglican churches in the greater Norwich area, as well as the non-Anglican churches, and via the local press, it invited written contributions from the general public. It also looked at the role of the Cathedral, but stopped short of giving it parochial responsibilities.

The Report concluded that that only six of the 31 mediaeval churches were needed for worship: four large parishes (St Peter Mancroft, St Giles on the Hill, St George Colegate and St Peter Parmentergate), with the two extra churches, both within Parmentergate, of St Julian (owing to its unique nature) and either St John de Sepulchre or the extramural 1840s church of St Mark, Hall Road. In the event, for a number of reasons, 14 were left open (those in bold are the 'super-parishes'; the others were to form part of them in due course):

St Peter Mancroft
    St Stephen;
St Giles on the Hill
    St John Maddermarket

St Andrew
　　　St George Tombland
　　　St Helen
　　　St Mary-in-the-Marsh[6]
St George Colegate
　　　St Augustine
St Peter Parmentergate
　　　St Julian
　　　St John de Sepulchre
　　　St John Timberhill.

The Report was, of course, concerned mostly with living churches and parochial responsibilities, and less with the actual buildings, although it did pay some attention to the problem:

> The Commission sympathises with the widespread feeling that every one of the redundant mediaeval buildings should be retained. But if they are to be retained, some new means of financing their upkeep must be found. The Church in Norwich has not got the resources to do so.[7]

The fate of the redundant churches was to be decided by the Pastoral Measure of 1968. If no appropriate use could be found (which involved selling or leasing the church to its new occupant), and if it did not qualify for financial assistance from the Redundant Churches Fund (RCF),[8] a church was at risk of demolition. The RCF would take on only the very best churches, and most of the Norwich ones did not come within that category: although there are some excellent buildings, the importance of most of them is as part of the collection. The international importance of the collection was noted, but the Commission concluded that it could 'hardly presume to recommend in way the people of Norwich should seek to preserve their heritage'.[9] It came up with a list of 'wholly suitable' uses, and opined that a commercial use which preserved the building's aesthetic integrity was more acceptable than a social use which obscured it, but that is as far as it went.

Both these ideas – the dispersal of ownership, and even more, demolition – shocked the community deeply. Following the publication of the Report, a voluntary organization was set up under the leadership of the indomitable Lady Harrod, the Friends of Norwich Churches, with a base in St Mary Coslany, which raised a good deal of money and carried out some immediate remedial repairs to some of the buildings. The Friends was wound up in 1986, and members were encouraged to join the Norfolk Churches Trust.

Alongside this, the Lord Mayor for 1970/71, John Jarrold, instituted a 'caretaker' scheme, whereby 'commercial and industrial concerns in the City have undertaken to look after the churches near their premises and to deal with minor repairs'.[10] It was a valuable, if temporary, means of preventing unnecessary decay.

Norwich Corporation (as it then was) found the Pastoral Measure to be unacceptable, and after various consultations, led by the then town clerk (later chief executive), Gordon Tilsley, Alderman Thomas Eaton and Councillor Raymond Frostick, it made an offer to the Church Commissioners to take on the freeholds of the various churches as they became redundant, which was accepted. It then set up the Norwich Historic Churches Trust

Figure 3 St Etheldreda, looking east. Photo by George Plunkett, 1937, reproduced by kind permission of Jonathan Plunkett. (Contrast with its modern appearance: see page 64.)

(NHCT) in 1973 to care for the unneeded ones, and to identify alternative uses for them. It was thus ensured that no church would be demolished, and that, in the words of the Policy Committee, 'all the churches shall be retained for future generations to enjoy'. This was welcomed by the Advisory Board for Redundant Churches,[11] which expressed the hope that other municipalities would follow suit. (This did not happen except in Ipswich; York deliberately chose not to follow the Norwich model.)

The NHCT was therefore incorporated on 17 September 1973, as a company limited by guarantee with charitable status, and the first churches were handed over in 1975. The City Council leases them to the Trust on 99-year peppercorn leases – this includes both the buildings and their churchyards.[12] Some were in a fair condition, having been used for worship until their closure, but others, which had been closed for longer, were in a very poor way, and a major programme of restoration and renovation was put in hand. In many cases, internal alterations had to be made in order to make them usable, but all such interventions are reversible, and do not obscure the beauty of the building.

The buildings have all been deconsecrated, so are technically no longer churches. The basis on which the Trust operates is that it is responsible for the repair, maintenance and management of the buildings, and has to raise the income to keep them standing and weatherproof. This has, in the past, been done partly by an annual grant from the City Council, and by grants from other sources, as well as rental income. However, all internal work, such as heating, lighting and lavatories, has to be provided by the tenants, in consultation with the Trust.

Since its formation, the Trust has considered a vast number and variety of applica-

Figure 4 St Gregory, looking east. Photo by George Plunkett, 1937, reproduced by kind permission of Jonathan Plunkett.

tions and proposals for its buildings. To be acceptable, proposals need to be both viable and appropriate, and involve tenants raising funds in order to meet the capital cost of adaptation where needed. It has a responsibility to seek new and suitable uses, in particular those which are for 'civic, public, or educational purposes, or for storage'. However, emphasis in recent years has been on lettings which will allow public access, either on spec or by arrangement, and there have been a number of very successful commercial uses which allow almost permanent public access, such as antique centres and bookshops. The Trust is currently the largest landlord in the city to arts-based organizations: ten of the 18 have such uses (see Appendix). As might be expected with such a large number of properties, there have been occasional problems over the years, including a couple which gained the Trust bad publicity at the time, but most are sorted out amicably.

The Trust comprises a number of trustees, with a part-time administrator[13] and a part-time surveyor of the fabric. The work of these last two has increased greatly in the last few years, and they are increasingly assisted by volunteers. Since 2010, the Trust has had its own office space in one of the churches (the two-storey medieval vestry attached to the east wall of St Peter Parmentergate) from which the staff work, rather than as previously from home. This also gives the Trust a physical presence in the city.

The trustees are appointed in two ways. Each year three are nominated by the City Council from among its councillors, who sit on the Trust as they sit on the various other committees (planning, housing and so on) of the Council. Some of these stay on once

Figure 5 St Martin at Oak looking east from the interior gallery (since lost). Photo by George Plunkett, 1938, reproduced by kind permission of Jonathan Plunkett. (Contrast with its modern appearance: see page 77.)

their term is over to become trustees in their own right. The majority of the trustees are appointed for the skills they can bring to the Trust's work. They currently include solicitors, architects and accountants, as well as those who have a general interest in churches. Until about five years ago, all discussions and decisions were taken by the full Trust at a monthly meeting; as this often led to meetings of over two hours, sub-committees dealing with property (lettings), repairs and development have been set up, which meet separately and report back to the full Trust, which then endorses (or not!) their proposals.

In 2009, a Friends organization was set up, which gives people with an interest in supporting the churches and the Trust an opportunity to be involved. Events include social occasions as well as visits to the churches, and these give an opportunity to raise funds for the Trust. They are currently relatively small amounts, but they do help to fund specific projects, such as restoring the important Norman Bros organ in one of the churches. The Friends have been instrumental in widening participation in, and knowledge of, the Trust's work. One trustee is nominated by the Trust to sit on the Friends' committee, and the chair of the Friends attends Trust meetings.

Many of the churches taken over by the Trust were in a poor state of repair. With limited funding, our main focus has been to ensure that all properties are structurally sound and watertight. The programme has been determined by the availability of funds in any one year, often – in the past – dependent upon grants from either English Heritage or the City Council. Additional income is derived from rents, other grants and donations. The former cover the Trust's modest management and administrative expenses, the insurance premiums on unlet churches and minor housekeeping repairs. We are wholly dependent upon grants

Figure 6 St Swithin, looking west. Photo by George Plunkett, 1938, reproduced by kind permission of Jonathan Plunkett.

and donations for all significant repair works. In as many cases as possible, we have improved the facilities at the churches, and as will be seen, insertions of mezzanines, galleries and the like have been made: all these are reversible, and do not impinge physically on the fabric in any way.

However, this modus operandi has now proved to be inadequate: the annual Council subvention of about £20,000 was withdrawn in 1990, and without major improvements to the facilities of several of the buildings (lavatories, heating systems, and even running water in three cases) they become ever more difficult to let, as prospective tenants quite reasonably expect adequate facilities. One of the sub-committees, originally set up to raise funds for improving four churches (St Margaret de Westwick, St Clement at Fyebridge, St John de Sepulchre and St Gregory Pottergate) eventually realized that the way forward was to cease piecemeal fundraising, and to apply for a major Heritage Lottery Fund (HLF) grant to cover work at all 18 churches. This resulted in a major reassessment of the way the Trust functioned which had continued effectively unchanged since its inception in 1973. In early 2014 two meetings were held, led by a heritage consultant. One meeting was for the trustees and members of the committee of the Friends, and the other for the tenants. The Trust is thus currently reassessing the way it functions, how trustees and officers are appointed, relationships with tenants and with the Friends, and its physical presence in the city. The way the Friends operate may well change as a result of this exercise, too. However, as Gordon Tilsley wrote in his report looking back at the first 20 years, 'we face the future with some concern, but not without hope'.

Appendix: uses to which the redundant churches have been put

The first date is that of closure and/or redundancy; the second is the date the church passed to NHCT.

All Saints (1973; 1975)
Ecumenical multi-purpose centre; then a place offering hospitality, with a focus on the less-privileged, until 2015. Also Mothers' Union office housed here 1989–2003. Now anticipated to become an offshoot of the antiques centre at St Gregory.

St Clement at Fyebridge (1971; 1975)
Rented by a Methodist minister and kept open as place of prayer and meditation until 1999. There was then a short occupation by the Romanian Orthodox congregation. Now used by a master mason as a city base for eight apprentices with an emphasis on teaching and attracting other young people into the craft.

St Edmund Fishergate (1950; 1975)
Store for cardboard box factory next door. Since NHCT: Scenery store for Puppet Theatre; a community church and pregnancy crisis centre; Call to Prayer.

St Etheldreda (1961; 1975)
Artists' studios since 1980, providing affordable studio space.

St Gregory, Pottergate (1971; 1975)
Community arts centre; events centre administered for NHCT by an agent; antique and collectors' centre.

St James Pockthorpe (1971; 1975)
Original home of the Night Shelter (see St Martin at Oak); Puppet Theatre.

St John de Sepulchre (1984; 1984)
Used by a congregation of the Exarchate of Parishes of the Russian Orthodox Tradition, for some years from 1984. Currently vacant.

St Margaret de Westwick (1974; 1974)
Gymnasium; now exhibition space administered for NHCT by an agent.

St Martin at Oak (1976; 1976)
Night shelter for homeless; briefly artists' studio; now Wharf Music Academy.

St Martin at Palace (1971; 1975)
Store for furnishings for Diocesan Furnishings Officer; Probation service and successors; Recently vacated and seeking a new tenant.

Figure 8 Advertising new uses: noticeboard at St Michael at Plea, Norwich. Photo by Steven Saxby.

Figure 9 The interior of All Saints, Norwich, then used as a cafe and daycare centre. Photo taken by Steven Saxby in 2013.

Figure 10 St Michael at Plea has a Christian bookshop in the nave and a cafe in the chancel. Photo (2016) by Susan Curran.

St Mary Coslany (1971;1975)
HQ of Friends of Norwich Churches; craft and design centre; publishing services company office; internet book business (with some space licensed to artists).

St Michael at Plea (1971; 1975)
Antiques and/collectibles centre; SPCK bookshop; independent Christian bookshop. In all cases with café in chancel.

St Miles Coslany (1971; 1975)
Scenery store for Puppet Theatre; martial arts gym, attached to nearby sports centre; 'Inspire' Science Centre; Lost In Translation circus training school.

St Peter Hungate (1936; 1995)
Museum of church art under City Council control 1936–95. Since 2008, Hungate Medieval Art, housing exhibitions of medieval and related art.

St Peter Parmentergate (1981; 1980)
Stood empty from closure until 2007, since when Norwich Academy of Martial Arts. (The vestry houses the NHCT office.)

St Saviour (1971; 1975)
Parish hall; badminton court; then evangelical youth club; diocesan furniture store; now Thalia Theatre Company.

SS Simon and Jude (1892; 1975)
Sunday school for St George Tombland 1913–20. Boy Scouts shop and centre 1952–97. Briefly a boxing gym. Now Anglia Academy of Dance.

St Swithin (1951; 1975)
Furniture store. Since NHCT: 'Premises'/Norwich Arts Centre, with contemporary music, art, etc.

Dr Nicholas Groves is a freelance lecturer and writer in church history. His previous publications have included The Medieval Churches of the City of Norwich *and* William Stephen Gilly: An exceptionally busy life, *the biography of a 19th-century clergyman. He is a trustee of the Norwich Historic Churches Trust.*

Acknowledgement

An original version of this article appeared in *Ecclesiology Today*, nos 49 and 50 (double issue), July 2014, pp 70–83. Much further information is from a report on the first 20 years of the Trust, produced in 1993 by its then chair, Gordon Tilsley; a small booklet published by the Trust in 1976; and the 1971 Report of the Policy Committee of the City Council regarding redundant churches in Norwich.

Notes

1. Lincoln had 72 churches. Thetford had 22, of which three survive, only one of which is still in use.
2. The authorities wanted to rebuild only 39 of them, but faced strong parochial opposition. See Paul Jeffrey, *The City Churches of Sir Christopher Wren* (Continuum, 1996), p 25 ff.
3. When St Lawrence came under the care of St Giles in 1973, it was discovered that the church had simply been locked after the final service in 1968 and left, with everything in place. Hangings fell to pieces as they were touched, books disintegrated, and everything was damp. (pers. comm. the late C. W. Risebrook of St Giles).
4. I recall visiting St Margaret de Westwick in about 1973, and being told by the churchwarden that the congregation was herself and one other person. The vicar was also vicar of Kirby Bedon, where he lived, and came in once a week. Two years later it was closed.
5. Norwich City Commission Report.
6. St Mary in the Marsh was another anomaly. The parish covered the Close, but the church was demolished by the dean and Chapter in 1568. The congregation worshipped in a number of places, latterly St Luke's Chapel in the cathedral. The parish was finally dissolved in 2016.
7. Report, p. 22.
8. Now the Churches Conservation Trust (CCT).
9. Report, p 23.
10. Report of the Policy Committee, p. 3.
11. Succeeded in 2007 by the Statutory Advisory Committee on Closed and Closing Churches.
12. Although the churchyards are leased to the Trust, the City has long had the responsibility of maintaining them, under the Closed Churchyards legislation. They were closed as burial grounds in 1854.
13. Officially executive officer and company secretary.

The Norwich Historic Churches Trust, returning churches to the community

Rory Quinn

Introduction

What follows is partly history and partly a description of what the Trust encompasses and tries to do with its responsibilities. I shall give particular prominence to items of which I have first-hand knowledge, as someone who has a long association with the Trust and has recently been its chair. I was also a City councillor between 1969 and 2004.

The Council of the City and County of Norwich took great pride in its role of acting for the community. There seems to be a long history of all parties acting closely together to promote the best interests of the citizens and trying to provide a very high standard of service to them. This pride was reflected in the interest it took in all parts of the life in the city, including its ecclesiastical buildings. Norwich City Council first took on a redundant church in 1523, when it leased St Mary the Less for 500 years and used it as a cloth hall. This was a period rather like the present when there was a major reorganization of parishes, with some churches being made redundant and many demolished.

Henry XIII's reign brought the closure of monastic institutions, and the City took on a number of ex-ecclesiastical buildings to protect the services they provided. The Carnary College became the King Edward VI School, the Great Hospital which looked after the elderly was given back to the City by Edward VI, while the City had to purchase the Dominican friary to ensure it was kept for civic use. Now known as St Andrew's and Blackfriars Halls, it is used for concerts, markets and public and private functions.

Some churches became redundant in later eras. St Peter Southgate was demolished in 1887, and proposals to demolish SS Simon and Jude at about the same time were fiercely and successfully resisted. It became a church hall and then the scouts centre.

The 19th century saw the construction of large factories in the city centre and the disappearance of the gardens that had been a major feature of Norwich. Terraces of houses filled any space available. The 20th century saw major measures to improve housing and the start of large-scale slum clearance. In Norwich the focus of attention was the housing in the yards of the old city, which was replaced by new housing estates on the edge of the built-up area. The population of the centre fell rapidly, and the need for so many churches disappeared.

When St Peter Hungate was proposed for redundancy, the City converted it into a museum of ecclesiastical art in 1936, the first such use in the country. Other church buildings had effectively become redundant as they were no longer used as parish churches, and one was usefully turned into a store for a shoe factory. John Betjeman featured this in a television programme, *A Passion for Churches,* which was made in 1974, three years before the Trust received any of the churches. It did not make an inspiring sight, and large amounts of guano had to be removed from the base of the tower before anything else could be done with it. Another church featured in the programme was St Mary Coslany,

Figure 1 Plaque in St Peter Hungate, Norwich. Photo by Susan Curran

which had become a furniture store. The only community use was in St Lawrence, where artists were going about their work. When this church was made redundant, it was briefly looked after by the Trust. The then sheriff, Norman Lake, led a successful campaign to raise funds to repair the south clerestory, which was threatened with collapse.

A few of Norwich's medieval churches were destroyed during the Second World War. St Julian however was rebuilt, using some of the surviving original fabric.

The first recent issue concerning church redundancy related to a 19th-century church, St Philip, Heigham, which was at the bottom of Stafford Street on Heigham Road. It had been built to serve its suburb, and dominated it physically. When it was declared redundant, the City Council worked with a housing association to produce a scheme to convert the nave and chancel into housing. This proposal was rejected by the Norwich diocese, with the canon responsible demanding that it be demolished. The Council was dismayed by this attitude but had to accept that the Church of England had the last say in this matter. It did ask that the diocese consider retaining the tower, as it played such an important role in the landscape. The redoubtable canon is believed to have said that he was not going to live in his new vicarage in the shadow of a church tower! The tower was demolished along with the church.

This skirmish caused considerable concern , and this grew into major alarm when the diocese proposed to make redundant over 20 medieval churches in the city centre. It turned out that the alarm was felt not just by many in the city, but also by the Church Commissioners, who were concerned that the Norwich diocese was not following their own guidelines.

The Brooke Commission

A commission was set up to reorganize the parishes in central Norwich (within the line of the medieval city walls) under the chairmanship of Lord Brooke of Cumnor. It reported in

1969, and proposed to create four parishes, with the majority of the existing churches to be declared surplus to requirements. The town clerk, Gordon Tilsley, with representatives of the two political parties, Tom Eaton for the Conservatives and Raymond Frostick for the Labour Party, considered the way forward. The City's response was to open discussions with the diocese, and a report was drawn up. It recommended the setting-up of a new trust to find new uses for the buildings and to care for them. The Council considered the report and accepted the recommendation on 5 October 1971.

A group was established to take this proposal forward. The diocesan representatives were led by a member of the Brooke Commission, the vicar of St Peter Mancroft, Canon Bill Westwood, whose constructive approach was greatly welcomed. I was somewhat surprised to be nominated to the it as one of the Council's representative by a rather mischievous Councillor Patricia Hollis.

The first meeting of the new Norwich Historic Churches Trust took place on 21 July 1972. The trustees appointed Mr W. R. (Rowan) Hare as their chair. He had been the chair of the Friends organization which had been created in response to the proposal to make so many churches redundant. The Council agreed on 21 October 1972 to make a grant of £1,000 towards administrative costs and an annual capital grant of £10,000 for five years to cover repair costs.

The physical state of the buildings was poor, since little maintenance had been done for a long period. This huge backlog of repairs was to be a challenge for the new body, and it continues to be so today.

One of the objectives of setting up the Trust was for the city to make use of at least some of the newly available buildings to provide new facilities for its citizens. The trustees explored a range of possible new uses with this remit in mind. The Museum Service was asked to consider extending its activities into some of the churches. Francis Cheetham, its director, responded by focusing on those that were near existing museums. St Gregory and St John Maddermarket were near to Strangers' Hall, while St Andrew was close to the Bridewell. Consideration was given to using these buildings to house much of the Museum Service's extensive collection of artefacts. These included a major costume collection, the third largest in the country. It was suggested that most of this be located in St Gregory, with the extensive collection of ecclesiastical costumes going into St John Maddermarket. St Andrew was considered for housing 'farm carts, large farm implements and transport', items that are now at Gressenhall, but it was acknowledged that the 'church was to continue in use for some time'. In all this review listed nine churches for particular uses and three more as of interest.

Unfortunately most of these proposals were taken no further. The one proposal that was pursued was to create a costume museum in St Gregory. A scheme was drawn up whereby the City Council would make a substantial contribution to help put the building in repair, while English Heritage would assist with a further grant. Norfolk County Council's intended contribution was to fit out the building as a costume museum, and plans were drawn up to this end. There was a major public debate, in which I took part on behalf of the Trust.

The publicity this proposal received led to suggestions of other uses for St Gregory. The owner of the nearby shop Head in the Clouds put forward a proposal to establish a music venue there. Michael Cartiss, the chair of the Museums Committee, asked the

Figure 2 The lower-level art studios (the staircase at the end leads to a mezzanine) at St Etheldreda, Norwich, 2014. Photo by Susan Curran. (Contrast with the photo on p. 52.)

chief executive of the County Council if the County was legally obliged to carry out the costume museum scheme . He was advised that it was not, and in response the County withdrew from the scheme, effectively bringing it to an end. (The music venue proposal was taken forward.)

One of the considerations made at each new application for use is its appropriateness in view of the former status of the building. We were advised by one of our trustees, Canon Bishop, that the nave of a church had historically been a space for the congregation to use as they wished. He joked that parishioners had rood screens built to keep the priest out of their part of the church building. This brought it home to trustees that they need not be too precious about the uses of church buildings, as historically they had been used for all sorts of purposes. Medieval churches effectively replaced the secular halls which had been a feature of Anglo-Saxon settlements, and took over many of their uses. We are lucky that a manorial screen survives in Strangers' Hall showing what a secular screen looks like with the more important person having some privacy with his lady. The Cathedral was no exception, and the City Council used to finish its mayor-making by repairing to the Cathedral for a jolly good nosh up. It is a tradition that is due for revival!

Over a period of time, what we would now call non-religious uses were driven out of the naves, and communities had to find other venues for them. In due course the state found that the churches were the ideal network for state propaganda. A historian remarked that after all the Church of England was the first nationalized industry – and of course it was a state monopoly, just as subsequent ones were.

Medieval churches had little fixed furniture, so the bare state of most of the buildings that the Trust inherited was closer to their original state than the pew-filled buildings (typically with Georgian or Victorian fittings) which we are more familiar with today. It is interesting to note that the Church of England is now clearing bench pews from the naves of many of its parish churches, so the space can be used more flexibly by the community. 'Loos not pews' was the slogan that came out of a conference held by English Heritage in St Swithin about the way forward for all churches. Community use is now seen as the means of making the buildings relevant to the communities they serve. The recent renovation of St Stephen (in conjunction with the development of an adjoining shopping mall) is a good example. The church has been transformed by the changes, and is now used much more extensively than had previously been the case. However, this kind of transformation calls for (and in this instance it received) a large investment.

The Trust takes an interest in what happened to the furnishings in each church, whether they have been removed before handover or not, and tries to keep track of their current whereabouts. Bells remain in some of the towers but most peals have been stripped out. We regard them as part of the fabric of the church, and we were particularly upset to find that the historic peal in St Gregory had been removed and melted down for money before the building was vested in the Trust. The frame remains. The bells that made up a fine peal at St John de Sepulchre were scattered around the diocese and the frame was removed, although efforts are being made to recover it. The peals at St Miles Coslany and All Saints remain in place, and they are still rung on occasion.

The trustees

There has always been an attempt to keep a balance among the trustees. There are those who provide professional oversight, such as architects, surveyors, solicitors and accountants, and those who represent the wider community interest. At the beginning there was a conscious attempt to include all the main strands of Christian belief, and some trustees fitted more than one category. Comparatively recent additions to the expertise have been a historian and a landscaping expert.

The Council has the power to nominate some trustees. I was among those initially appointed in this way. Some Council appointees have continued their service well after their initial nomination period, such is their interest in the work of the Trust.

The churchyards

The churchyards were always envisaged as community space, and a complement to the sparse amount of public open space in the city centre. This is laid down in the leases to the Trust from the City Council. They are maintained by the City, as had been done previously under the Closed Churchyards legislation, and this obligation is repeated in the leases. Although they were all originally intended to be public open spaces, sometimes restrictions on access have been implemented by the City to reduce nuisance. This has never been done by the Trust.

In a few cases local groups have contributed to the design and layout, adding flowers and shrubs of their choice. The Norwich Society has contributed bulbs and its members' time. There is much more that could be done to engage the local communities in their care. Recently a scheme to link all the city centre churchyards and create walks between them, called Heavenly Gardens, was devised by George Ishmael, a landscape gardener who is one of the trustees. It has received some funding for its development and implementation, but needs far more if it is to be fully realized.

Inevitably, as the churchyards are all in the city centre, they are also used for less pleasant purposes. Collecting used needles from some of them has to done regularly. Even more alarming, some sexual assaults that have taken place in their dark corners. The Trust has tried to take action with the City to reduce this risk. Considering the size of the night-time economy and the tens of thousands of people thronging the city at night each week, we are have got away lightly so far.

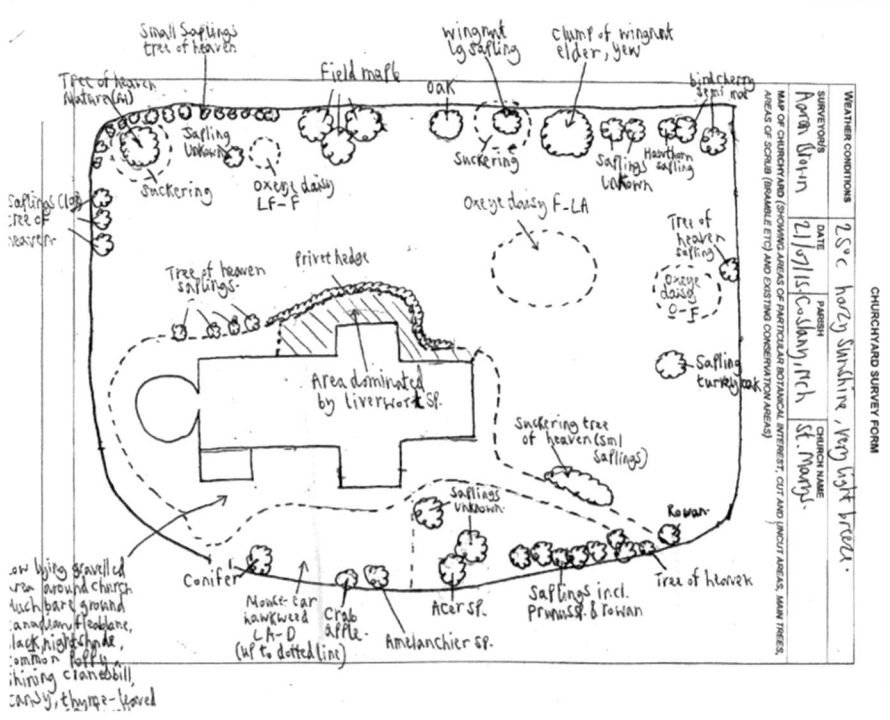

Figure 3 In July 2015 the Norfolk Wildlife Trust (NWT) made surveys of St Margaret Westwick, St Mary Coslany (shown above) and St Michael Coslany as part of its Churchyard Conservation Scheme in conjunction with the Heavenly Gardens project (www.heavenlygardens.org.uk). The work will continue in the summer of 2016. Plan drawn by Aaron Brown.

The churchyard of St Peter Hungate has been relandscaped as part of a scheme to resolve problems with the neighbouring premises, the Briton's Arms. The link between the two buildings has been re-established and the original churchyard wall on the north and west sides uncovered.

Doubt was expressed about the status of the churchyards to two churches made redundant before the main group, St Peter Hungate and SS Simon and Jude. A City Council officer suggested that the churchyards had not been deconsecrated. The architect of the Norwich Preservation Trust, which was renovating the Briton's Arms, was persuaded to make an application to the Diocesan Board for permission to make alterations to the churchyard, and was asked to pay a fee. This prompted further research which showed that both churches had gone through the same redundancy procedure as the remainder of the portfolio, and the churchyards were deconsecrated as well as the churches. Although this incident was annoying at the time, it helped to clarify the situation. Scrutiny of the basic legislation showed that the Church of England had only been granted delegated powers from Parliament over its own property, and all orders had to be endorsed by Parliament before they had any power. The Church has no powers over the churches that are no longer its property or their churchyards, and the issue of consecration was in fact a red herring.

Funding

When the Trust was launched, the City Council provided funding both for the administration of the Trust and for a modest repair programme. It was intended that the buildings be leased to tenants to provide a further income. However when the churches were first let, they were basically shells with no facilities except for electric light. The rents they commanded were correspondingly low, so they brought the Trust little income.

Rent concessions were given to tenants who committed to investing in the buildings, and through this means some of them gained basic facilities. Some of these improved buildings were surrendered to the Trust, and this gave the Trust churches to rent with decent facilities which of course could command more significant rents. Over time this process built up, and now the rents provide a more than nominal amount of income for the Trust.

In 1986 when Gordon Tilsley was chairman of the Trust, a major fundraising effort was launched. The Appeal Committee was chaired by Richard Jewson. Ken Rowe was approached successfully to be the appeal director. For two years he worked with a secretary in a Norwich Union office just off the Marble Hall with no monetary award for himself or his secretary. Potential patrons were approached on the basis that each could open doors either directly or indirectly to funds. The Appeal Committee members were approached on a similar basis and became a very active team. Mr Rowe said that he thought the appeal had run its course when people started crossing the road in the main shopping street to avoid him. The appeal lasted two years and the sum raised acted as a lever for further funds, particularly from English Heritage, the total in all being about half a million pounds. This allowed much work to be done to the fabric of St Michael at Plea in particular which allowed SPCK to move in and other problems to be addressed. He subsequently became a trustee.

Over time, and as pressure on its budget increased, the City cut and then ceased its annual grant to the Trust. It continued to provide some funding for repairs from its Conservation budget, although the amount was erratic. This funding too ceased when that budget was closed down. Since then the City has made a number of one-off contributions to capital projects, but it makes no contribution to the Trust's operating expenses. Fundraising for specific projects has continued to be pursued by both the Trust and its tenants.

The Trust allocates a budget annually for minor repairs and for a contribution to major schemes, which can realistically only be pursued with outside support. Major repair and improvement projects typically cost £100,000 or more. Structural repairs have been carried out on roofs and walls, but the largest expenses have generally been for the repair of towers, which is often essential for safety reasons. The prominent towers of St John de Sepulchre and St Miles have received extensive repairs over in the last few years, with the latter, our largest project to date, costing several hundred thousand pounds.

A normal business would expect a return on investment, but this is not realistic for the Trust. Although improvements to church facilities are typically reflected in increased tents, structural repairs, especially to towers, yield no financial return, and are carried out as part of the Trust's general remit to maintain this vital part of the city's heritage.

English Heritage has given generous support to the major projects, and at their request a Conservation Management Plan was prepared to cover ten years of maintenance proposals. The Trust budgets a sum of money each year to contribute to the cost of these major capital schemes but English Heritage provides the majority of the funding. Minor repairs can be equally essential, but it has proved much more difficult to obtain grant funding for these, and the cost typically has to be met out of the Trust's own funds.

Unfortunately as part of the recent drive for austerity, English Heritage (now Historic England) has had its budget from the government slashed by 53 per cent, which made it impossible to continue to give grants at the same level. It is possible still to seek grants from the Heritage Lottery Fund (HLF), but the HLF has quite different criteria, with an emphasis less on conservation than on community benefit. Dialogue is continuing, and the HLF has recently made a significant grant for activities designed to meet the Trust's educational objectives and increase its profile, but there is an urgent need for continuing funds to meet maintenance and repair obligations.

Conservation of art works

The church buildings in the Trust's care contain works of sculpture in stone and wood, wall paintings and some stained glass. Many are medieval but the memorials for the most part are from later periods. The finest wall paintings are in St Gregory. When the large painting of St George and the Dragon was discovered in 1861 it was literally front page news in the national papers. Further paintings were discovered in 1979 and an expert from the Victoria & Albert Museum regarded them as the finest 15th-century wall paintings in England. The City was then at its richest and its burghers could afford the best. The Trust commissioned conservation work to help preserve them. St George and the Dragon is still quite dark, as the conservators were very conservative in their approach and did not want to risk losing any original paint. A painting of it made when it was first uncovered in the 19th century shows details which are difficult to make out today, including the

RETURNING CHURCHES TO THE COMMUNITY

Figure 4
Painting made of the large wall painting of St George and the Dragon in St Gregory, done when it was uncovered.

tower of St Gregory's itself. The other surviving painting are of three of the four doctors of the church including St Gregory, St Ambrose, St Jerome (the fourth, St Augustine of Hippo, is lost) and one of the Annunciation.

St Miles has medieval wall paintings with later writing over them, but these have been overpainted. It is probable that other paintings also survived under the whitewash in the churches, but no comprehensive investigation has as yet taken place.

The Trust commissioned a report on the monuments in its care, and instituted a programme of works to consolidate those most in need of work. Although several outstanding monuments have benefited from conservation work and can be better appreciated as a result, as always there is much more that could and should be done if funds permitted. Special mention should be made of the 1623 Berney monument in St Peter Parmentergate. This features two recumbent figures in contemporary costume, and remarkably, the design of their surround includes two native American faces. The Pilgrim Fathers made their voyage to North America in 1620 with East Anglian among them. The restorers used the lettering recorded by the historian Francis Blomefield to guide them in renovating the text on the monument where there was doubt about what it read.

Some items were removed from the churches at the time of redundancy and rest in the care of the Castle Museum, and others have been relocated in other churches.

Uses

The Trust has sought community uses for the buildings whenever possible, but with such a large volume of churches to be tenanted, it is difficult to find community uses for all of

Figure 5 Wall painting of St Ambrose in St Gregory, after conservation in 1999 by the Perry Lithgow Partnership. Illustration kindly provided by Mark Perry.

them, so tenancies have also been granted for commercial purposes. All tenants commit to make the buildings accessible to the public at least on an occasional basis. Although storage is an option, it has been avoided for the most part. Some uses have continued for a considerable period, while other tenants have come and gone. The majority of churches have been let, and are contributing positively to the life of the city.

The uses have been wide-ranging. Most are secular but some are religious. The Norwich night shelter moved from St James to St Martin at Oak, where it was located for many years before finally moving to purpose-built accommodation. After adaptation, this building is now used for music teaching.

RETURNING CHURCHES TO THE COMMUNITY

Figures 6 and 7 Wall paintings in St Gregory, after conservation in 1999 by the Perry Lithgow Partnership: above, the Annunciation, left, head of St Gregory. Illustrations kindly provided by Mark Perry.

Figures 8 and 9 Details of the Berney and Hobart monument in St Peter Parmentergate when dismantled for conservation. Photos by the author.

Figure 10 Several churches have stained glass, from the medieval period onwards, most notably St Peter Hungate (here, from the East window). Photo by Susan Curran.

The congregation at St Clement was greater than that at St George Colegate at the time when church redundancies were being considered, but presumably because St George is architecturally the more distinguished, it was chosen as the parish church and St Clement was made redundant. This church retains many of its furnishings, which makes letting it a more complex process. It was taken on by the Rev. Jack Burton, a Methodist ministe who lives opposite. He kept the church open as a place for quiet reflection (and occasional services) for many years. The annual Mathew Parker service is still celebrated there, and the church is now the centre for the Stonemasons' Guild.

Norwich Community Church took on two buildings, St Saviour and St Edmund Fishergate. It too has now moved to purpose-built premises in the shape of the King's Centre in King Street, opposite the Trust's small office in the vestry of St Peter Parmentergate. St Saviour is now tenanted by the Thalia theatre group, and St Edmund houses Call to Prayer. The Russian and Romanian Orthodox churches occupied St John de Sepulchre and St Clement for brief periods. Neither have good facilities, and St John was at the time of writing being considered for a new use.

The creation of Norwich Puppet Theatre was a project that received the full support of the Trust. St James had been the original home of the night shelter. When it moved on to St Martin at Oak, the project to take over the buildling was led by the remarkable Tony Ede. It involved the construction of a theatre largely for children, respecting the historic fabric. He used the project to train young people in construction skills, and was very proud when all of them went into full-time employment. The DaSilvas were the puppeteers, and created the only such theatre outside London. It has survived considerable vicissitudes and is going strong again thanks to a new board, although funding is always a worry for such organizations.

The Norwich Arts Centre has been a long-term tenant of St Swithin, occupying both the church building and the original church hall, which has been much extended and improved. While the Trust is delighted with their success, it has proved very difficult to negotiate with them as tenants. If all our tenants were as difficult as they have been, the Trust would have collapsed.

Art is also well represented, with St Etheldreda being used as studios and St Margaret as a gallery for temporary exhibitions. Both buildings have lacked some basic facilities, although recently progress has been made in installing a simple kitchen and lavatory at St Margaret. Both sets of tenants have had to suffer for their art in the winter months, as they have no heating.

Martial arts have been catered for first in St Miles and then in St Peter Parmentergate. St Miles was used for science education for quite a long period, and a circus school has recently taken over the building. St Gregory was used for music performance for some years, then as an arts centre, and is now an antiques centre. St Michael at Plea had also been used for that purpose before SPCK took it over.

The Science Centre in St Miles helped young people get a greater understanding of science in its many forms but eventually ran out of support from sponsors. The City Council had invested in it to create a martial arts venue attached to its Duke Street centre next door. One of its students later created his own martial arts centre at St Peter Parmentergate.

The probation service converted St Martin at Palace Plain into offices, and its successor

Figure 11 Preparing for an event run by the Friends of the NHCT at St Edmunds, Norwich (tenanted by Call to Prayer), 2011. Photo by Susan Curran.

organization worked there until the government changed its tendering process to a regional one, so that local organizations were unable to tender any more.

One proposed use was for a drinking establishment modelled on the lines of the one depicted in the American film *Coyote Ugly*. This is a coming of age film about a young woman, set in a bar with all-female staff. The plans submitted for this project in SS Simon and Jude seemed satisfactory, with the main bar being on the site of the original altar. Our administrator was keen on the idea of female empowerment. I decided to check on the film, and found that one scene was definitely likely to raise eyebrows if it was repeated in our building: the staff danced topless on the bar. I approached the person who was said to be the main backer to get assurances about the supervision of the conduct in the bar, and learned that although she knew the person we had been dealing with, she was unaware that she had been named as a backer. Needless to say this proposed intriguing but rather questionable proposal did not go ahead.

Tenancies

It takes a special person to take on premises as unusual as a church, and we have been fortunate that so many potential tenants have seen the special qualities of the buildings, and appreciate them as much as we do. On the whole the landlord-tenant relationship works well, but problems can and do arise. Rent reviews sometimes cause tension, but most problems arise when the tenants themselves run into difficulties.

Figure 12 Searching for a use: St John de Sepulchre, located at the edge of the city centre, and without a water supply, sanitation or heating, has proved a difficult church to let. Photo taken in 2014 by Susan Curran.

One remarkable tussle over a tenancy occurred over St Michael at Plea. The Society for the Promotion of Christian Knowledge (SPCK) had taken a tenancy and installed a bookshop, investing in fine fittings in the nave. A restaurant was set up in the chancel. Unfortunately SPCK began to lose large sums of money in its bookshop operations and decided to end this part of its mission. It conveyed its premises, including this lease, to two Americans who promised to make the shops profitable. In fact this was not entirely the intention: we discovered that the pair intended to use the building to promote a church called St Stephen the Great, which had an anti-Islamic slant. We were informed by our solicitors that there was nothing in the lease to prevent the assignees from converting the building back into a church of this denomination. We have now added a clause to our standard lease to prevent this happening in future.

SPCK had certainly not envisaged this outcome, and was very cooperative in helping us resolve the matter. The Trust was eventually able to break the lease because the new assignees declared an intention to have it administered by an organization based in Texas, while our leases require tenants to be based in the UK. As an interesting postscript, we were sent as a document detailing the judgement made against one of these American in a bankruptcy case. He was ordered to pay various sums and to complete ten hours of 'Continuing Legal Education' including a minimum of two hours on ethics.

In the wake of this, the Americans removed all the stock from the shop and restaurant, then returned to remove all the furnishings, leaving only items that were bolted to the fabric such as the bookcases. One of my more unusual tasks as chair of the Trust was to monitor this process and make sure they did not remove any of the property of the Trust. The Trust had kept in touch with the SPCK's manager, Steve Foyster, and happily he was able to bring together interested parties to form a body whose objective was to continue with the Christian bookshop and revive the restaurant. This new body took on the lease, and the operation was successfully relaunched.

Colin Pordham, a solicitor by background, was the chair of the Trust before me and its secretary before that. He pointed out that an enormous amount of time is spent on considering applications for use, and very few reach fruition. Often there are long negotiations with those proposing possible good uses, which are ultimately unsuccessful . As a result churches stand empty for long periods, waiting for a use that does not materialize, with consequent loss of income to the Trust and disappointment for the public which wishes to see the buildings used and if possible accessible. Another problem is that some people expect the Trust to hand over buildings for no or very little rent, especially if the prospective tenant is another charity. It is not consistent with our obligations as a charity, nor is it financially practicable, for us to do so.

The City Council has advised the Trust that it should look to lease some of the churches to commercial tenants who will provide a basic solid reliable income. The Trust has tended to give preference to community uses, but the organizations involved frequently have financial problems, and it is a particular problem when a tenant fails to prioritize payment of the rent. Although the Trust does its utmost to be a good landlord, it has an obligation to obtain the income necessary to keep the buildings in good repair, since this is its core charitable objective, and it is sometimes necessary to take firm action as a result.

Two of our tenants that ran restaurants as part of their operations found that they were making unaffordable losses. There are heavy costs to the Trust in terminating a lease and seeking a new tenant (with often months or years of negotiations between tenancies), so in one case the Trust made rent concessions to try to help the organization keep going. Unfortunately when a consultant was employed to help plan a way forward, serious maladministration was discovered. This was an issue that should have been picked up by the charity's trustees. The Trust suffered unwelcome bad publicity when it concluded that it had no option but to terminate the lease. The building was relet to the same organisation after it had sorted out its problems. The other charity closed abruptly when it found it was trading while insolvent, which is illegal, owing the Trust large amounts of money, and again blaming the Trust for its problems entirely without justification. It is very difficult in these situations to put across to the public the need for the Trust itself to act in a businesslike manner, even when its tenants are deserving charities.

Although the buildings in the Trust's care are deconsecrated, the Trust consults the Diocese of Norwich when a religious use is proposed for them. The first such enquiry followed the proposed closure of the Roman Catholic chapel in Fishergate to allow industrial development. The congregation expressed an interest in moving to St Martin at Palace Plain. We were somewhat surprised to learn that the bishop was not in favour, and was reported to have said that he did not want Rome on his doorstep. More understandable was the bishop's rejection of the Liberal Progressive Jews as a possible tenant. I learned from one of the Church Commissioners that it is official policy for the Church of England to discourage the use of former church buildings by non-Christian religions.

One building that got away was the wonderful Old Meeting House. It was to have come to the Trust, and was included in its early literature, but difficulties over the lease meant that the transfer never took place. The City Council has kept the building in repair, but it has never had the kind of use that would bring the Norwich public in to appreciate its very rare qualities. It remains in limbo as I write, with its small congregation unhappy with their situation.

Another redundant church over which the Trust has been consulted on is St Mary the Less, which is in private ownership. We continue to hope that in future it will be placed with the Trust or another conservation body.

Education and history

One of the current trustees, Dr Nicholas Groves, produced a new and more comprehensive history of Norwich's medieval churches, including those that have disappeared. This has provided a sounder understanding of this part of our heritage. Dr Groves has also led walking tours of the churches which have been well received. For some time he represented the trustees on the committee of the Friends of the Norwich Historic Churches Trust, which holds educational events including church tours and lectures as well as fundraising activities. The Trust and the Friends together organized one-day conferences in 2014 and 2015 (with another planned for 2016), and selected papers from them have been published in two volumes, of which this is the second.

A major academic study is under way led by the UEA of all the medieval churches of Norwich. This too will deepen our understanding of them and highlight their importance.

Website

The Trust was actively considering setting up a website when a happy encounter with Frances Holmes led her and her husband Michael to grasp the opportunity. Both Frances and Michael are local historians as well as web developers, and were keen to contribute to bringing this part of the history of Norwich to a wider audience. The Trust cares for just some of the medieval churches of Norwich, and it was decided that the website should embrace all of the churches. It contains details of all 31 surviving churches, and includes a glossary of terms used to describe these buildings. Michael and Frances researched the individuals behind many of the monuments and memorials, and were able to identify portraits of many of them in the Castle collection. This information about prominent members of the congregations gave a human dimension to our appreciation of the churches.

The enormous amount of work that went into the website gave Michael and Frances encouragement to research and publish on other aspects of Norwich history. The Trust is now looking at updating the original site, retaining much of this valuable information, but ensuring that the site provides up to date and readily accessible information on the Trust and its activities, and is linked in content and style with the website recently set up by the Friends.

What of the future?

Major reviews of the Trust's activities have taken place to produce a Conservation Management Plan and to review its governance. Previously reviews led to legal services and letting services being put out to tender, and this brought about changes in both areas.

Figure 12 A barbecue and concert held by the Friends of the Norwich Historic Churches Trust in 2015 at St Martin at Oak, Norwich, now occupied by The Wharf music academy. Photo by Susan Curran.

Norwich's medieval churches have made a continuous considerable contribution to the life of the city, and the aim of the Trust is to ensure that they will continue to do so in the future. Although these buildings are public assets, government restrictions in local government expenditure and the cuts to Historic England's budget mean that the Trust will have to look elsewhere in the future for contributions to its finances. I hope this volume will contribute to the efforts to make the people of Norwich aware of this tremendous community asset, and of the urgent need for funds to preserve and enhance it for the future.

Rory Quinn was a long-serving member of Norwich City Council, and after many years as a trustee of NHCT, became its chair from 2004 to 2015. He is also a member of the Norwich Society, chairing its Conservation and Development subcommittee, a director of the Norwich Preservation Trust and a member of the executive of the Friends of Norwich Museums.

Heavenly Gardens

George Ishmael

It is impossible to walk through Norwich city centre without passing an ancient church. At every turn, a church tower, a flint wall, window tracery or churchyard railings seem to work their way into the view. The churches are indeed a characteristic feature of the city; one which led to the old saying that Norwich had 'a pub for every day of the year and a church for every Sunday'. Even this was something of an understatement, but incredibly 32 medieval churches survive, endowing Norwich with a unique collection of pre-Reformation churches; more than anywhere else north of the Alps.

Every church, of course, has a churchyard, and these small green oases, scattered throughout the city centre, play an important part in the street scene of Norwich. For example, churchyard trees are prominent in many views and in a city of narrow streets and lanes; they characteristically add greenery to areas that would otherwise be dominated by buildings.

The churchyards together comprise some 5 hectares (over 12 acres) of green space, making up a considerable proportion of all open space in the city centre. Unfortunately, however, many are difficult to access and some are even permanently locked. Generally, they are hemmed in closely by neighbouring developments: a legacy of the Victorian industrial era when every bit of available space within the city walls was crammed with housing or industry.

Fortunately, the sensitive redevelopment of neighbouring properties can open up these spaces to public view and allow them to breathe again. The regeneration of the former Caley/Mackintosh chocolate factory, for example, created a new space, Chapelfield Plain, which together with the adjoining churchyard of St Stephen's now attracts thousands of people a day to an area that was previously inaccessible to the public. The retail development at Chapelfield provided the funding to revitalize the churchyard, with new boundary walls, paths and planting. Artists Wolfgang and Heron were commissioned by the developer Lendlease to produce attractive new gates and railings. The church itself has also become more visited because of the improved access and attractiveness of the churchyard. The parishioners and other local groups have become involved in gardening activities around the church. Regular bedding-out of annual flower displays is carried out with the help of City College students with learning difficulties, who grow the plants from seed at the College. This community effort contributed to the Chapelfield area winning the Urban Regeneration category in the 2008 Britain in Bloom awards and the 2009 international Communities in Bloom. More recently, the use of annual bedding has tended to be replaced by a more sustainable approach employing perennials. This might not produce as much bold colour, but it makes for a longer season and more emphasis on shape and texture. In addition plants adapted to drought conditions can be used to reduce inputs of precious water.

The churchyards thus represent a rich resource, and when circumstances allow they provide a productive focus for community effort. They assume an increasingly important

Figure 1 Wildlife surveyor Aaron Brown checks out the churchyard of St Mary Coslany. (All photos by the author.)

Figure 2 Part of the drought-resistant garden at St Stephen

role as the resident population of the city centre increases, and it is evident that local residents, either individually or in groups, often take a great interest in the maintenance of the churchyards, as wildlife havens and as spaces to sit or garden.

It is tempting to imagine Norwich's ancient churchyards as a series of attractive gardens, full of people and activity: groups of schoolchildren learning about their environment; young people learning horticultural skills; tourists being guided around; local residents relaxing amongst plants and works of art. What a change this would be from the present situation of largely unused, inaccessible and often dull spaces around the churches.

The diversity of control of Norwich's medieval churches (spread between the Norwich Historic Churches Trust, the Churches Conservation Trust, the City Council – largely for the ruins – and the Diocese for the eight working churches), together with the statutory responsibility of the City Council to carry out regular maintenance of the churchyards, illustrates the difficulty of getting a focused approach to the development of the churchyards as a valuable community asset. The churches are all Grade I listed buildings, and as such deserve to have an appropriately attractive setting.

The existing community effort needs to be united and given the support it deserves to ultimately realise the vision offered by the Heavenly Gardens proposal. This aims to develop and promote the churchyards of Norwich city centre, collectively, as a botanic garden consisting of a series of separate gardens linked together by pedestrian walks. I have led several such walks over the past year, each one linking four or five churchyards and of no more than an hour's duration. They were all enthusiastically received, and the participants were surprised to discover little known alleyways and lanes in the heart of the city, as well as an impressive range of trees, including species of Celtis, Nothofagus, Euodia, Gymnocladus and other unusual specimens. Currently a series of self-guided trail leaflets is in preparation, linking up all of the medieval churchyards.

The churchyards provide sheltered sites for a wide range of trees, shrubs and perennials, which could be developed along various themes, such as the dye plants used in colouring the cloth during Norwich's heyday as a centre for the weaving industry. Currently the churchyard of St Margaret on St Benedicts Street is being developed as a medieval garden using only plants available before 1500. These were essentially herbs with a practical use in the home, the infirmary or the workplace. Many were native plants brought in from the surrounding countryside. No doubt there is an endless array of possible horticultural themes, including scented gardens, national collections of appropriate plant species, or heritage related designs.

The churchyards could be a very visible showcase for environmentally sensitive practice, and demonstrate how people could look after their own urban gardens with due attention to contemporary issues such as water economy, recycling and biodiversity. In this respect there are already some interesting examples of churchyard management in other parts of the United Kingdom. The churchyard in the village of Bolton Percy near York, for example, has been densely planted with herbaceous perennials, to stunning visual effect.

A number of wild flowers in Norfolk depend heavily on churchyards for their survival, and there is every reason to believe that these can be encouraged into the city churchyards. To this end the Norfolk Wildlife Trust is surveying the churchyards (see page 66) to identify what is growing there and how a greater diversity of native plants can be encouraged to thrive.

Figure 3 A Heavenly Gardens churchyards trail

The western edge of St Stephen's churchyard has had nearly ten years of consistent management to encourage spring-flowering wildflowers under the trees and a summer flowering meadow in the more open area near the Chapelfield development. An information board explains the management approach to visitors. A similar approach is taken in St Giles churchyard, with more decorative perennials at the front of the church by the main entrance and a wildflower meadow at the rear, which was originally created at the request of adjoining residents who have no gardens of their own.

The churchyards also lend themselves to the provision of appropriate sculpture as focal points for the design. Some interest and sculptural effect is, of course, provided by surviving monuments, although most of the old headstones seem to have been removed early in the twentieth century to make grass cutting easier! Old tombs, where accessible, are often used

Figure 4 Perennial ground cover in Bolton Percy churchyard

Figure 5 Volunteer gardeners in St Margaret's churchyard

as seats, but it would clearly be better to introduce some attractive bespoke seating, as at St Gregory and St Stephen.

Creating a botanic garden in the city centre churchyards will not require expensive infrastructure such as roads, car parks, cafes and other visitor facilities – they already exist! Furthermore, there is a ready-made audience or customer base already living and working in the vicinity. The immediate objective is to create a showpiece churchyard (at St Margaret's) to demonstrate the advantages of the Heavenly Gardens approach and to enable further fundraising. It would also be appropriate to find space in one of the redundant churches that can display a permanent exhibition describing the history of the churchyards and showcase the plant collections within them. Such a venue could also act as a base for guided walks, talks, fundraising activities and so on.

Figure 6 The wildflower area at St Stephen

The Heavenly Gardens project has a number of objectives: to develop the churchyards for the enjoyment of the general public and visitors; as a focus for community activity; as a contribution to the cultural life of the city; and as a resource for environmental education and horticultural skills training.

Initially it was intended to establish a new trust, with charitable status, to raise funds and achieve these objectives. It was clear, however, that they are complementary to those of the existing Norwich Historic Churches Trust, so the initiative is hosted by that organization. Other trusts have happily participated, such as the Town Close Trust which has given grant aid for a pilot project and the Norwich Society, whose members have volunteered to provide and plant spring bulbs. And, in a city famous for nonconformist views, other churches such as those of the Quakers are also participating. The Quaker Meeting House in Upper Goat Lane, for example, has recently developed a 'quiet garden' where everyone is welcome to come and have lunch, read a book or sit in contemplation. It won the Best Churchyard award of Norwich in Bloom in 2015.

In 2014, The Norwich Society published a survey of the churchyards, calling them 'hidden gems' that were underused and under-appreciated. The report confirmed that although they were reasonably well maintained by the City Council, a lot more could be done to be inventive and increase their use. One of the ideas suggested was 'grassless lawns', which have been pioneered by researchers at Reading University, and involve the planting of diverse low-growing plants which can literally be mown like a lawn but provide colour and wildlife interest around the year.

There are no end of good ideas that could be developed: perhaps something along the lines of the Museum of Garden History near Lambeth Palace in London; or the churchyards could become an extended sculpture park; a sheltered learning environment; or a combination of all these things and more. There could surely be a bright future for the city-centre churchyards as a vital and much cherished part of the City's heritage and social life.

George Ishmael is a chartered landscape architect, currently promoting the 'Heavenly Gardens' initiative. He spent 35 years with Norwich City Council, leading on landscape issues, and is now a trustee of NHCT.

Notes

If you would like to get involved with the Heavenly Gardens proposal, please contact George Ishmael, tel 01603 504368 (eve) or preferably by email <georgeishmael@hotmail.com>.

The self-guided walks leaflets are available from the Tourist Information Centre, located in the Forum.

For more information

See George Ishmael, 'Heavenly Gardens', *Norfolk Gardens Trust Journal,* Spring 2010. The Heavenly Gardens website is at www.heavenlygardens.org.uk

Confessions of a former tenant

Susan Curran

I first thought about leasing a redundant medieval church in the winter of 2001. I'd just been looking at an upper-floor former hairdressing salon as a possible office for my small publishing services business, and deeply depressing it had been, as had been all the small premises I'd looked at. We edit, typeset, proofread and index books for publishers worldwide: it's a business sector that has been hit hard by third-world competition, and we could only afford a relatively low rent. But there had to be something available that we could become more enthusiastic about, surely; somewhere that would not make our hearts sink at the prospect of spending long hours working there.

I had been a trustee of the Norwich Historic Churches Trust for about ten years at this point. I'd been appointed by Norwich City Council when I was a councillor, and had stayed on after I left the council. I knew from experience how difficult the Trust found it to identify satisfactory tenants for many of its churches. The trustees had been discussing St Mary Coslany, a large edge-of-city-centre church which had been vacant for several years, only a few days earlier. And heading back to our temporary office from the wretched salon, I thought, would my colleagues think me mad if I suggested we move to St Mary?

We had been in temporary accommodation, much too cramped and not a viable long-term option, since we had been burgled out of our previous office in Swan Yard, Norwich a few months earlier. We'd loved Swan Yard, but since the burglars had ripped out an entire barred window, the police were at a loss to suggest anything affordable we could do to make the premises more secure, and a repeat burglary about a month later had almost sent the business under. It had fallen in size to just three staff: myself, my husband Paul Simmonds who worked with me part-time, and my old friend Chris Carr. But I hoped to rebuild the business to its former size of half a dozen or so, and I wanted to find premises that would be secure and offered some space for expansion.

A redundant medieval church was not the obvious choice, I knew, but it thought it was worth a look. And as well as being conscious that it wasn't what my colleagues would be expecting, I knew that my company didn't rate as an ideal tenant for the Trust. In an ideal world, it would let all its churches to well-resourced charitable organizations that provided a community benefit and plenty of public access. The perfect tenant would also have a hefty sum to invest in providing modern facilities and adapting the premises (in a reversible way) to its new use. But it has never been possible to find 18 such tenants in central Norwich, so the Trust had long been willing to consider most proposals, including some that would have raised eyebrows a generation ago, such as martial arts centres and bar/restaurants. If I and my company took on the lease, the Trust would get a tenant who cared deeply about Norwich's medieval heritage, understood the Trust's own position, and would be committed to paying the rent promptly (which is not true of every tenant, in the past or indeed now). I didn't take it for granted that my fellow trustees would say yes, but I though there was a fair chance.

Although the Trust has always used property agents to try to find tenants, my personal

Figure 1 St Mary Coslany, Norwich. Photo taken in 2008. (All photos by the author.)

impression has always been that it's a task for which they show limited enthusiasm. Commercial agents used to conventional offices and warehouses seem to find it a little difficult to work out which of their enquirers might usefully be directed to a redundant church. They present relatively few potential tenants, and quite a few tenants have come through other routes instead. When I asked (through the Trust's then administrator, Colin Bodkin) to view St Mary's, the agent who showed me round made it pretty clear he didn't expect me to make an offer on the premises, and I confess I could see his point. The hairdresser's salon would have fitted into St Mary's a dozen times over. If you stacked it vertically, make that twenty times. The church had the dull air of a place that has been long unoccupied. The previous tenants (who had run an antiques and collectibles centre and a small café) had left a miscellany of junk strewn around it, and there were dead birds and a whole shoreline of small-scale trash and muck. The agent's details were rudimentary: as I recall they didn't extend beyond a very rough floor plan and a note that subject to planning permission, the premises would be suitable for a variety of uses. It took a major leap of imagination to see the building as an office for a small group of editors and typesetters.

I went back to Chris and Paul and reported as honestly as I could. That is, I said that I thought we'd probably be mad to take on St Mary, but even so I was tempted to do it. I was enormously heartened when Chris's response was 'Let's do it, then', and Paul backed him up.

We wanted to move quickly, because we had to leave our temporary premises very soon, and Colin Bodkin and the trustees were also very supportive. They agreed to grant us a six-month licence, starting on 15 December 2001, which would enable us to move in while a full lease was negotiated. They also, crucially, agreed that although we could not sublet the premises, we could introduce other occupants on a licence basis that did not give them any security of tenure.

Reader, we took it.

Just prior to Christmas is not the ideal time to move office into a filthy medieval church. We spent much of the holiday period clearing out the junk (bar a few chairs and shelves which I salvaged: years later I met the previous tenant, and squared the deal by paying her a token sum for them) and filling a skip with it. Generous friends helped us, and if they thought us mad, they kindly refrained from saying so.

We paid to have the windows cleaned, too – by a specialist firm, after many local window cleaners turned us down. It cost a fortune, so we only did it the once.

The lease

I remained a trustee of the Norwich Historic Churches Trust when I became a tenant, although of course I did not participate in any decisions that directedly affected my company. I felt it was desirable for there to be a representative of Norwich's small business community on the Trust, and also desirable for there to be first-hand experience of being a tenant.

At Swan Yard our 'lease' had been two sentences long, and worked fine, but the Trust – perhaps unavoidably for a charity – used solicitors who submitted to us a lengthy lease full of boilerplate clauses. The Trust does not demand full repairing terms, probably because no tenant would be willing to take them on. Among the clauses that gave me pause, however, was the one requiring us to decorate the entire premises every five years. Someone somewhere must have noticed that this was a medieval church, since it did specify limewash: but does any church get limewashed from top to bottom every five years? If one does, it was not St Mary, I'm afraid.

Agreeing the rent for a church is also difficult: another tendency of agents is to work to a fixed per-square-foot formula that doesn't easily fit this kind of atypical building. St Mary had very mediocre facilities, and a location that (as the antiques people had found) didn't rate as prime city centre, so the rent (about which, as a trustee, I could not haggle too hard) was reasonable. But as well as high power costs, churches have high insurance costs (which are passed on to tenants), so the overall costs of occupying the building are greater than the headline rent might make them seem.

The church

St Mary is not the most elegant church in Norwich. It is blessed with a fairly low round tower that arguably dates from around the Conquest, which is attached incongruously to a 15th-century perpendicular church. There are no aisles, just one large internal space; two short transepts, the north one containing a kitchen area of sorts; and a chancel that is quite a bit lower and narrower than the nave. The entrance is via the south porch, which has a modern door at its exterior and the original medieval door inside. There's a small room over the porch, which the previous tenant seemed to have used as an office. I found it very claustrophobic: the only entrance was via dirty and crumbling spiral stairs, and we

Figure 2 The author's workstation, with the glorious monument to Martin von Kurnbeck to the left. Note the electric radiators, including one tactically positioned under the desk. Plants (see left especially) grew very well.

used it only for occasional storage. Two loos were set at the base of the tower (cleaning these was the very worst job when we moved in), and above them, wooden stairs led to a tower room, opening via a stone arch to the body of the church, which proved to be easiest place in the church to license out. An iron ladder led up the tower, with a shallow parapet around the top; I fear I never found the courage to climb it, though many friends did over the years.

A small door in the chancel, which we normally kept shut and rarely used, provided a fire exit.

The only stained glass is of roughly Edwardian date, mostly heraldic shields, but there are battered angels decorating the crossing (the then clerk of works claimed to have the missing wing from one of them) and an interesting, if a little short of distinguished, collection of monuments. They originally included one to Peter Lingcole, dated 1298, in Norman French, which we searched for at length when a visitor arrived seeking what he claimed was the earliest known memorial to an ancestor of Abraham Lincoln. Alas, it was not there; it was suggested to us that someone at the university had taken it away, and I have no idea of its current whereabouts.

I set up my own work station by the chancel monument to Martin von Kurnbeck, a Hugenenot doctor I believe, of 1579. It's interesting because of the contrast between the elegant canopy surround and the very sketchy figure incised into the stone within it, almost like a cartoon for a relief figure that was never put in place (or if it was, has been

Figure 3 The north side of the nave. Note the heating/lighting units (not all of which worked) high up on the walls, and the mess of wiring around the edges of the kitchen (right). The monument to the left is the one mentioned to Thomas Daniell.

long since lost). Over the chancel on the south side a small 16th-century family kneel either side of their parents, but I felt more fondness for Ann Claxton in the north chancel, with the ill-spelled details of her huge family (14 children) and little hedgehogs in the corners of the brass plate. I also spared a few thoughts for the Rev. Thomas Daniell, an early nineteenth-century voyager who died a long way from home, and whose slab in the nave laconically quotes Job: 'He shall return no more to his house, neither shall his place know him any more.' That's almost as depressing as the one in St Miles Coslany just round the corner, which records nothing about its subject except that she fell down dead while conversing with her husband in the street.

The office

It is perhaps as well that publishing companies have a reputation for bohemianism, since our office at St Mary could certainly be described as bohemian. Some rather raggy grey carpet covered the chancel floor when we moved in, and we retained it for a while, before deciding it was so disgusting it was better junked, covering the worst patches with old rugs. We placed on it our selection of second-hand furniture and cast-offs retained from the clear-out. It was not really practicable to put anything on the walls (though we did erect a whiteboard with our planning schedule), bar some posters attached with blu-tak. Some potted plants introduced to cheer the atmosphere grew expansively.

Figure 4 Plan A to solve the heating crisis: a heavy lined pair of curtains installed by theatrical curtain specialists. The office is behind them in the chancel; the nave is filled with an internet bookseller's stock. Note too the fine roof, much repaired particularly after wartime bomb damage.

It was a pleasure to have a generous workstation each, something not true in our previous temporary quarters. With careful placing, we did not have too much trouble from light falling on our screens – which otherwise could have been difficult, since it was not an option to curtain the windows. Although the photos might suggest otherwise, we are all pretty tidy individuals, and things were kept in good order. Our clients very rarely visited, which was perhaps as well.

The cold

Most of the formalities of moving in – such as getting planning permission for our new use and getting a phone line installed – went smoothly and quickly. The electrical system caused us a few more problems: it had been installed in a very chaotic way, with cables trailing unappealingly all up the church from board and meters in the north-west corner of the nave, and needed some work before it provided adequate power in the chancel, where we had decided to set our office. We were very conscious of the responsibilities of occupying a listed building, but the electrics – visually, as well as functionally – really weren't of Grade I standard. A friend created a temporary wooden cover to hide the meters, which improved the appearance significantly.

The main problem was, and always remained, the heating. It is unfeasibly expensive to heat a huge, high-roofed medieval church to an ambient temperature suitable for an office. The rather rusty steel boxes that punctuated the walls about 12 ft from the ground proved to be combination heating and lighting units. Most of the lighting worked, though we were warned that if any (more) of the elements died, they would probably prove impossible to replace. (We used desk lamps to supplement this rather patchy source of light.) Some of the heating elements worked too, but 1) the heat was barely discernible at ground level, and 2) as soon as we switched one on, we could see the electricity meter whirring around at top speed. The antiques people had left behind a couple of paraffin heaters, but we didn't think much of those: they were smelly and ineffective.

We invested in calling in a heating engineer (who worked, ironically, from another, but less ancient, redundant church in the city) in the hope of useful advice. We emphasized that we could not spend a fortune installing a new system, and that we thought the current system impossible. It would have been kinder if he had admitted he had no other proposals, but instead he charged us several hundred pounds for advising us that the only option was a replacement system on the same lines.

Our first attempt at an affordable solution was to hire an industrial space heater. It chewed up quite a lot of the available electric power in the chancel, but the main problem was the noise. It growled so loudly that whenever the phone rang we had to switch it off. It also created a fearsome draught. It was quite effective if you stood in the blast of hot air that came from it, but that was incompatible with actually doing work. We returned it pronto.

Our longer-term solution – to the extent that we found one – had two parts. First, we bought oil-filled electric radiators which we tucked into the kneeholes of our desks – probably to the horror of any fire inspector, but they did prove a little island of relative warmth in which each of us could work – and second, we paid for a heavy pair of curtains to be installed across the chancel arch. An attractive deep blue, they were fitted by a firm which specialized in theatre stage curtains. It took two men three days to put them up, and they only charged us around £500, so they must have made a serious loss on the job. In the summer we pulled the curtains back, but in the winter we kept them permanently closed, and groped our way through the gap between them when we needed to make a cup of tea in the transept or to go to the loo at the far end of the church. There was an appreciable temperature differential between the chancel and nave as a result.

For a while we also used gas-fired patio heaters to provide some more ambient heat. An insurance assessor who checked out the church demanded that we junk them. I still cannot see that they were a significant fire risk, and we grieved at their loss.

My team of workers were very gallant in putting up with an office temperature that must at times have dipped well below the legal minimum. My colleague Mike swore by fingerless greengrocer's gloves. One summer we had a student from southern Italy, Annalisa, seconded to us by an European work experience scheme. As it was summer it seemed to us quite comfortable in the church, but poor Annalisa found it arctic.

For the nave, we never found any good solution. Early on, a small company that did administrative work connected to trade fairs licensed the space from us. They moved in in the early summer, and I couldn't imagine how they would survive the winter. Since the company folded before winter came, we never found out.

The internet bookseller who has used the nave for some years now runs his business from inside a kind of plastic greenhouse. Although not visually appealing, that seems at least to be a functional system.

The happy side-effect

We never got sick. I mean, never! In the six and a half years that we occupied the church, not a single member of staff ever took a day off ill. We didn't have colds. We joked (and it was probably true) that any germs any of us brought in must have died in the arctic wastes that separated each one of us.

The animals

I had no problem sharing our working space with skeletons, and turned down the offer from one early artist licensee to exorcise the building, since I never sensed any unquiet spirits there. (She was invited to leave after I found her sleeping overnight in the tower room.) But I had not anticipated when we moved in quite what an array of wildlife would share the church with us.

Figure 5 A touch of whimsy from an artist licensee

Death watch beetle treatment was carried out a few months after we moved in, and for a few days we had to vacate the church while it was done. No smell was noticeable after we returned, but the muck was: for literally years afterwards, the previous occasional sprinkling of muck from the roof became a steady shower. Not just dead beetles (though there were some of those) but a heavy black silt descended on our desks, rugs, computers, everywhere. It is not feasible to keep a medieval church as clean as a modern house, and we were realistic in our expectations, but the mess from the roof was a significant problem for quite a while.

The birds were a problem too. There were initially some gaps between the eaves and the roof, and for a while we regularly came into the church in the morning to find birds flying around. Even leaving the

Figure 6 The south side of the chancel c. 2008 – winter, since the curtain is drawn. Edwardian stained glass and a 16th-century monument are visible. This area was licensed out to a printmaker, whose heavy machinery is below the window.

doors open it was all but impossible to coax them out again. The Trust's jobbing builder, Steve Capper, did a valiant job of trying to stop up the gaps, but at its memorable worst we had half a dozen birds circling over our heads, which was seriously disconcerting.

The squirrels, although less frequent, were if anything even more disconcerting. I recall spending much of an afternoon trying to rig up a route to coax down a squirrel that had settled itself on top of the lighting unit above my desk. Perhaps it could simply have jumped, but it looked like a long way down, and it showed no inclination to do so. Our broom-pole passage clearly didn't tempt it, and we left that evening with the squirrel still staring beadily down at us. It was not there the next morning, and we never discovered a corpse, so presumably somewhere it found a route out again.

Security and visitors

We had no burglaries at St Mary. The previous tenants had left the rudiments of a burglar alarm system, and a friend spent quite a lot of time trying to make it work again (although perhaps it never had?) with total lack of success. But I think the main reason for our security was that no one knew we were there. The windowsills were all high, so no one looking from outside could see our desks and equipment.

From another perspective, that people didn't know we were in the building was in itself a problem. We did put a company sign on the main door, but delivery men frequently despaired of finding us, and it became routine to issue detailed instructions whenever we ordered office supplies. 'But there aren't any buildings on St Mary's Plain!' one frustrated DHL man wailed to me from outside. 'Try the huge one right in front of you' was my suggestion. Another phoned to say 'I seem to be in the porch. What do I do now?' The inner door was not locked …

Particularly memorable was the time when my colleague Sarah went out of the office at lunchtime, only to be stopped by a policeman demanding to know what she was doing in the evacuated zone. It turned out there had been a local bomb scare, and the police had evacuated everyone in the area – but it had never occurred to them that there might be anyone in the old church, so they hadn't alerted us. They suggested we should go outside and wait by the low wall opposite. After a short debate we concluded that if there was a bomb, we were likely to be much safer within the thick flint walls of the church.

We were always happy to open the church on Heritage Open Days, and to show other people around by arrangement. The Round Tower Society was among those who made appointments to view. Occasional unannounced visitors could be more of a problem. Indeed, the Norfolk Churches website (http://www.norfolkchurches.co.uk/ – no connection to the Norwich Historic Churches Trust) still announces that 'They keep it locked, and don't welcome visitors – indeed, when [a photographer] tried to photograph the inside, a rather pompous woman told him that she was "far too busy to keep an eye on you" and shut the door in his face, which seems a pity.' That pompous woman would be me. I think this was the man who rang the bell (we did have one) one Sunday morning when I had come into work after a long week because I was chasing an impossible deadline. I couldn't have let him in without pausing work to supervise him (since our licensees were worried, with some justification, about possessions going missing when we left people to roam about the building), so I apologetically explained that it wasn't an appropriate time to visit without warning. During the week in working hours the building was never locked, and indeed it wasn't on this occasion, although the door was certainly closed.

Although we initially laughed at those who joked that it would happen, we did indeed have visitors who rang our bell to gain access to 'the funeral' (which was actually at the Baptist church over the road) and others who demanded to come in and use our loos, on the assumption that any church, even a redundant one, is a kind of public property.

The vandals

It was a particularly sad day when I went into St Mary one Sunday to find a litter of glass all over the floor. Vandals had thrown stones targeting the stained glass shields, all of which were badly damaged. We saved the coloured glass fragments (which the restorers later reused, working from photos of the church before the damage occurred) and saved the stones we found too. I hoped the police might try to get fingerprints off them. But the police seemed to judge that there was no realistic prospect of solving the crime, and although the incident costs the insurers several thousand pounds, they never collected the stones or visited to investigate.

The rave

We were rather touched, in first clearing up, to find under a loose stone a little note in a matchbox commemorating the 'first rave' ever held in St Mary – unofficially, I assume, in the days when it was vacant. We didn't hold a subsequent rave, but we did hold a couple of great supper parties in the church, setting up tables across the transept and on one occasion feeding a three-course meal to about 30 friends (all dressed up for the occasion) using two elderly microwaves and a portable two-ring electric hob.

The licensees

Once we had occupied the chancel, and let out the tower room, it was more of a problem to find licensees for the rest of the building, even at very low rents. The heating problem meant that only the very hardy would have wished to use it for anything other than storage. We licensed space to a number of artists, including one who took the whole nave to display his large circular abstract paintings, and never seemed to come there at all. (He didn't last long, alas.) But we only found a long-term solution to the nave problem when our friend Keith Razey decided to set up a business selling second-hand books over the internet. Keith and his books took up most of the space, although an assortment of artists continued to (and still do) squeeze into spaces around him. When after six and a half enjoyable but freezing years I decided to slim the business down and retreat to working at home, Keith took over the lease of the building, and he remains the tenant as I write.

A last word

When I was a child I wanted to live in a castle. That is an ambition I am now never likely to fulfil, but it was a delight to be responsible for a while for my own round tower. I loved the expansiveness of St Mary and its echoing calm. Our office was a very quiet one (too quiet for a marketing specialist who worked with us for a while; he said he felt embarrassed to break the silence by phoning customers). For all its inconveniences it's a wonderful place, and I'm very glad to have had the opportunity to spend time there. I also feel it has much enhanced my value as a trustee: that first-hand knowledge of the problems tenants can face is irreplaceable. But those artic winters really were a burden, and I must confess I'm glad I shall never have to endure another one.

Susan Curran is managing director of Curran Publishing Services Ltd, and runs its publishing imprint, the Lasse Press. She has also written many books, including three medieval biographies, The English Friend, The Marriage of Margery Paston *and* The Wife of Cobham. *She has been a trustee of the Norwich Historic Churches Trust since the early 1990s.*

Inspired by the past – engaging the present – securing the future
New uses for religious heritage at the Churches Conservation Trust

Peter Aiers, Matthew McKeague and Edward Walkington

The Churches Conservation Trust (CCT) cares for the third largest historic estate in charitable ownership in the United Kingdom, a unique and ever-growing collection of nearly 350 Grade I or II* historic churches. The collection is diverse, ra nging from considerable town-centre churches such as St Mary in Shrewsbury (Figure 1) and St Thomas in Bristol (Figure 2) through to more modest, undiscovered rural gems like St Mary, Hardington Bampfyle, Somerset (Figure 3), and St Thomas, East Shefford, Berkshire (Figure 4).

The CCT was set up in the 1960s with a very specific remit: to preserve and conserve redundant Anglican churches with particular cultural, historical or architectural merit. Each of our churches is therefore remarkable in its own right. Our estate encompasses Saxon towers, Georgian follies and Perpendicular masterpieces; the earliest churches in cities of the Industrial Revolution, semi-ruins where only the tower still stands, and even a unique Puritan chapel completely unaltered (and almost entirely unused) since its construction in 1660 (Figure 5 – Guyhirn Chapel, Cambridgeshire). We look after churches from Cornwall's Roseland Coast to the foothills of the Northumberland Cheviots, but by far the greatest concentration of our estate is in East Anglia. We have 28 churches across Norfolk – more than in any other county – demonstrating the county's rich ecclesiastical heritage and historical wealth. This includes three in Norwich itself: St Laurence, St John Maddermarket, and St Augustine, which boasts Norwich's only 17th-century brick tower (Figure 6).

Core funding for the care of these churches comes from the Department for Culture, Media and Sport and the Church of England, but these sources of income are declining in real terms, while our estate grows ever larger. We faced cuts in funding of 20 per cent over the last Parliament, and the current economic turmoil means we cannot assume anything with certainty in terms of future funding.

We are meeting this challenge by stepping up our drive to raise funds through donations, commercial income and through innovative partnerships. We have been making strides in all these areas over the past few years: visitor numbers at our churches have risen and are now just shy of 2 million annually, and visitor donations have followed suit. But this still only accounts for a small proportion of our total financial needs, and we need to go above and beyond if we are to continue to achieve our aims to keep churches safe, welcoming to visitors and a focus for community life.

Figure 1 (above) St Mary, Shrewsbury. (All photos provided by the CCT.)

Figure 2 (left) St Thomas, Bristol

Figure 3 St Mary, Hardington Bampfyle

Figure 4 (right) St Thomas, East Shefford

Figure 5 Guyhirn Chapel

Figure 6 (below)
St Augustine, Norwich

Securing the future; learning from the past

Key to achieving this is the reuse or 'repurposing' of some of our historic churches. This can mean a variety of things, the simplest being increasing the number of events, services and open days in churches that have previously been little used. At the other end of the scale are major interventions and adaptations of churches where there are possibilities to work in partnerships with stakeholders, commercial businesses, local government, charities and a range of heritage organizations and trusts to regenerate the building, and to support the wider regeneration of the surrounding community. While the Trust's primary concern is and will always be the conservation and maintenance of our churches to the highest standards, we are also committed to enabling community groups in both urban and rural areas to use the buildings more regularly and for a wide variety of uses. This regeneration through practical projects helps to ensure the survival of the churches for future generations to enjoy.

Church buildings are usually at the physical centre of communities, but traditionally they were the societal centre too. The medieval church administered much of the modern state's remit – welfare, healthcare, education. Churches hosted the first vernacular theatre in Western Europe (medieval Easter plays), and were a hub not only of community but also of commerce – the first altar screens were erected to keep animals from wandering onto the sacred area.

Provision of such amenities gradually became the domain of the state, and as schools, hospitals and community centres opened, the community aspect of the church building declined. But in recent decades there has been a growing trend to look at how churches can begin again to provide spaces for a greater variety of uses, helping to ensure they not only survive but thrive in the 21st century. Our approach is to work with people to identify what their community's needs are, and to deliver projects that will meet these needs in what is likely to be their original community space.

First steps – Circomedia Bristol

The CCT trialled this approach at St Paul, Bristol, a late 18th-century gothic revival church with a wedding-cake tower set in a bosky Georgian square (Figure 7). Its surroundings had become increasingly run down, cut off from the city centre by a 1960s distributor road system. The Grade I listed church was vested with the Trust in 2000, by which time it was derelict and almost lost to the people of Bristol (Figure 8). Vandalized, stripped of many of its features and subject to antisocial behaviour, the future looked bleak: there were gaping holes in the roof, boarded windows, and a tower on the verge of collapse.

The task of repair was a big one, and unlike many of our rural churches there were few local people who still cared enough about the church to engage in large-scale fundraising. We needed a partner. Happenchance a nearby circus school, Circomedia, was looking to expand its operations and open a centre for aerial skills such as trapeze. It turned out our Georgian church, with its high, square ceiling, was eminently suitable for such a use.

A partnership was formed, and four years after vesting, with an HLF grant of £2.4 million towards a total project cost of £3.5 million, the church had been not only conserved but transformed. A sprung floor was carefully laid over the original, and the

Figure 7 St Paul, Bristol: exterior

Figure 8 (below) St Paul, Bristol: interior before renovation

Figure 9 Circomedia in action

Figure 10 Not just circuses – music performance at Circomedia

United Kingdom's largest indoor trapeze rig was hung from a rebuilt, strengthened roof (Figure 9).

Twelve years on, Circomedia continues to go from strength to strength, and is introducing a new Master's qualification in circus direction in September 2016. But its impact on the wider community is even more impressive. From the start, Circomedia has hosted community arts activity and outreach, alongside regular cultural events (Figure 10). This has kickstarted the regeneration of the wider area: Georgian terraces are being renovated for reoccupation, the streets are buzzing, and a neighbourhood once known for riots is fast becoming fashionable.

Going for gold: All Souls, Bolton

We are hopeful that a similar transformation will be the long-term impact of our second major regeneration project, in the North West. All Souls Bolton was a £5 million project that gave a new beginning for this important late 19th-century church designed by architects Paley and Austin (Figure 11). The enormous church was built for a large congregation in this densely built district of Bolton, but over the second half of the 20th century the area underwent demographic change and became a largely British Muslim neighbourhood. The congregation simply faded away, and the church, although structurally sound, was rarely visited and faced an enormous repair bill (Figure 12).

In 2007, local resident Inayat Omarji recognized the church's potential, particularly given the severe lack of community and business spaces in the surrounding area. He gathered support for the regeneration of All Souls and began to seek financial backing. In

Figure 11 The imposing exterior of All Souls, Bolton

Figure 12 (above) All Souls, Bolton's grand but neglected interior, before regeneration

Figure 13 (right) All Souls, Bolton: interior, after regeneration

Figure 14 All Souls, Bolton: heritage wall

partnership with the CCT, a rescue plan was developed which would breathe new life into All Souls, for the benefit of the whole local community: All Souls for all souls.

The sheer size of the nave, uninterrupted by columns, meant we could be ambitious: two modernist 'pods' have been inserted into the building, hosting workspaces, meeting rooms and a coffee shop (Figure 13). The main body of the church has been adapted to host large-scale events.

The architectural adaptations went through a rigorous consultation process which ensured the changes were appropriate and in keeping with the architectural environment of the church; while the adaptation is dramatic, the intervention retains the ambiance of the building including most of the fixtures, fittings and sight-lines. And like all our projects, the intervention was carefully designed to be reversible.

A key part of the project was to create a heritage wall with the local community which tells the story of the church, and of the surrounding area (Figure 14). We also supported local employment throughout the project. We offered six bursaries in heritage conservation throughout the project, and hosted craft skills workshops throughout the construction phase. Three of the six bursaries went on to long-term employment with the conservation building contractor.

All Souls, Bolton launched in August 2014, and initial results have been positive. A wide range of community activities and events are hosted in the centre, and a big success has been the business space. Demand for hot-desking space in particular has exceeded expectations, while meeting rooms are frequently fully booked. The community-run charity itself continues the skills focus by offering placements and training for underskilled young people in the surrounding area. The project has won several awards, including

Civic Voice's prize for best restoration project involving the community, and an English Heritage 'Angel Award' for the quality of the conservation work.

Building a sustainable future: St Nicholas Chapel, King's Lynn

Back in East Anglia we have delivered a project in King's Lynn, where the largest chapel of ease in the country has been conserved and transformed into an events space and visitor destination. This has been a partnership project with the Friends of St Nicholas Chapel, a voluntary group the likes of which are very important to our efforts in sustaining our churches and estate.

St Nicholas Chapel was built by the merchants of medieval King's Lynn as a demonstration of their wealth. Dating almost entirely from the late 14th century, it is a glorious light-filled exemplar of perpendicular, bound at each end by two enormous, delicate windows that let light pour into the nave under the longest of East Anglia's remarkable angel roofs (Figure 15).

The chapel later became known for its special link to the fishing community, the so-called 'North Enders' of King's Lynn, but as the fishing industry wound down, the chapel's traditional congregation moved away, and the building was eventually vested with the CCT. By the mid-2000s, rising damp and a poorly maintained roof had left the building in a sorry state, and its lack of facilities meant it was not being used to its full potential.

The building's magnificent unspoilt architecture meant a dramatic adaptation was

Figure 15 St Nicholas, King's Lynn: the longest angel roof in England

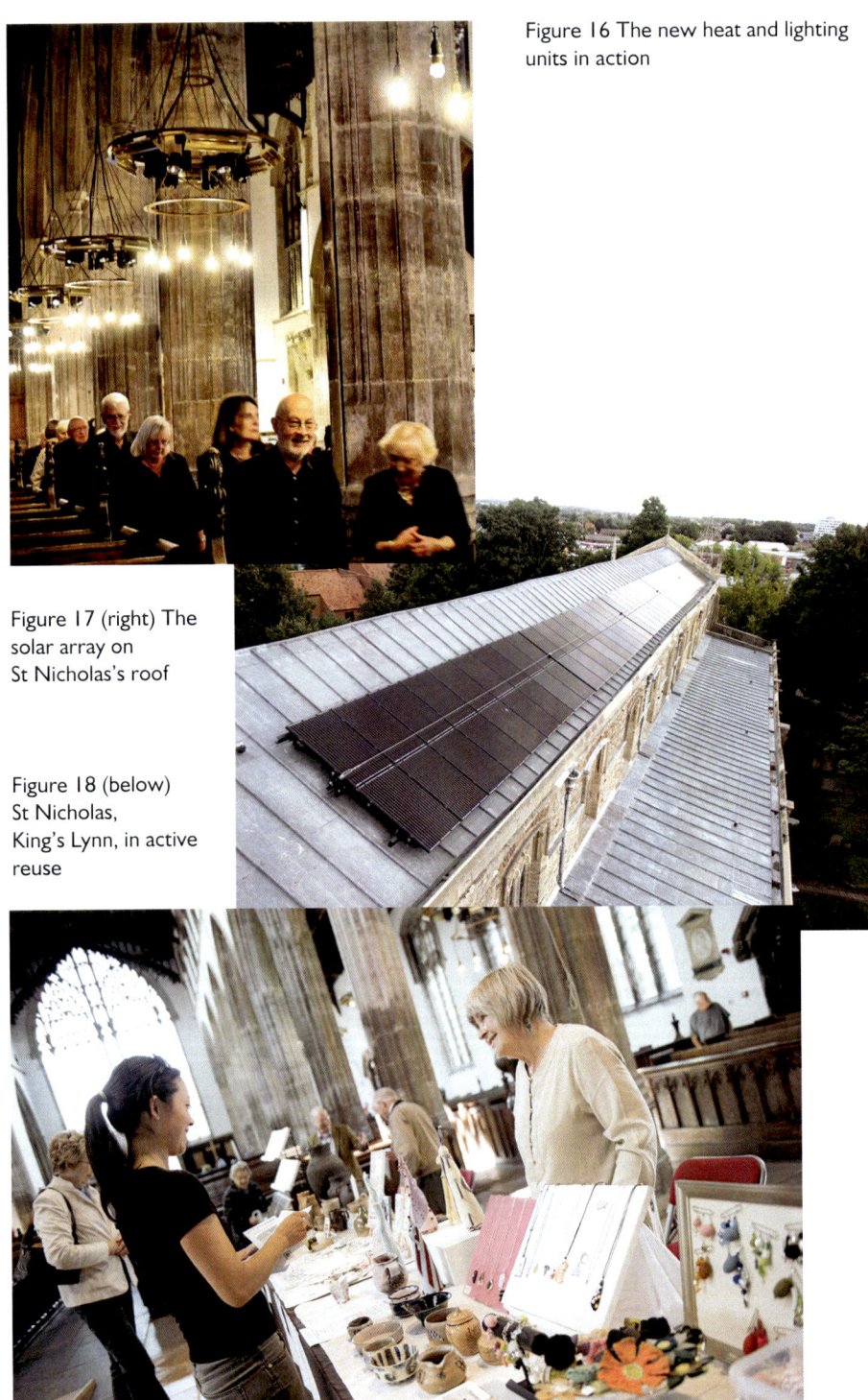

Figure 16 The new heat and lighting units in action

Figure 17 (right) The solar array on St Nicholas's roof

Figure 18 (below) St Nicholas, King's Lynn, in active reuse

never on the cards here, but we managed to squeeze toilets and a small kitchen into the base of its tower. The enormous space is heated from bespoke chandeliers which combine lights with radiant heat panels, far cheaper and less intrusive than traditional radiators or underfloor heating (Figure 16). But what makes the project stand out is its sustainability focus. Solar panels, invisible from street level, run the length of the roof (Figure 17), while water is recycled from rain.

The transformed St Nicholas Chapel opened in September 2015, and has seen a surge in visitor numbers well in excess of expectations, along with a growing number of activities and events (Figure 18). As I write in July 2016, December is already being booked up for Christmas parties.

Proving the link between heritage and wellbeing: Quay Place, Ipswich

Our next major project opens in autumn 2016. Another partnership project, this time with the charity Suffolk Mind, Quay Place transforms Ipswich's beautiful St Mary at the Quay into a heritage and wellbeing centre, bringing an innovative new use to a church that has suffered over the past 50 years through poor town planning. It was marooned amid dual carriageways and abandoned industrial buildings, its traditional congregation wholly vanished (Figure 19). Yet recent regeneration in the quayside area has breathed new life into the surroundings, with new businesses, housing, and the celebrated DanceEast moving in.

The start of quayside regeneration coincided with the realization that the building was fast becoming structurally unsound: the combination of the salty air and rising damp

Figure 19 St Mary at the Quay, Ipswich: inauspicious surroundings in the 1990s

Figure 20 (left) The crumbling pillars in St Mary at the Quay, Ipswich

Figure 21 (right) Approaching completion: the new extension in May 2016

Figure 22 (below) The new mezzanine provides structural support as well as meeting space

within the building, exacerbated by impermeable concrete pumped under the floor in 20th-century repair work, meant columns in the church were crumbling rapidly (Figure 20), and the south side had developed a Pisan lean. We reached out to the local community to identify a project that could attract funding to save the church, but also put it on a sound financial footing for the future.

Our search for a partner led us to Suffolk Mind who were looking for a unique building to develop a heritage and wellbeing centre that expands their offering to help encourage mental wellbeing for all. Over several years we worked out the shape of the final project, in close collaboration with the local community. One-to-one wellbeing therapies will be offered in a number of consulting rooms housed in a new extension designed in a sympathetic style (Figure 21). The original building will host group classes, a coffee shop and events, along with subtly inserted business and office space. In addition a wellbeing garden, to be maintained by volunteers, will be created on the south side of the church.

By extending as well as adapting the building, we have been able to leave the large nave – with its wonderful double-hammerbeam roof (the oldest in Suffolk) – largely unchanged. A sensitive modern mezzanine floor in the south aisle and gallery at the west end are the only insertions to the medieval structure, the mezzanine floor construction doubling up as support for the church's leaning pillars (Figure 22).

Quay Place is an ambitious, unique project, and it builds on an increasing body of evidence that suggests there is a link between wellbeing and connections to heritage. We shall be comparing outcomes of treatments at Quay Place with those at traditional centres for wellbeing services, not necessarily known for their architectural merit. Should the model prove successful, we hope to roll it out to other sites nationwide.

New ways of working with the community: the Common Room, Norwich

Further pilot projects by the Trust are planned. One that has been running in recent years took place at St Laurence in Norwich. St Laurence is a lovely large church, with an impressive long, tall nave, and a lack of pews which makes it more adaptable than many of our churches (Figure 23). Its location, however, on steep slopes leading down to the River Yare, means disabled access is a challenge, and it will be expensive to provide it with the services it needs to become a true community asset.

Our approach is always to offer something that is missing from a local area, rather than competing with established venues, and thus we were very conscious of the remarkable work the Norwich Historic Churches Trust has done to find new uses for its churches in the area. We knew we had to test something different.

In St Laurence's we ran the Common Room, a joint project with Civic Systems Lab and the University of East Anglia to test a new type of shared space, made and shaped collectively, and run on the principles of collaboration, connection and resourcefulness. Part of the EU-funded Heritage Recycle project, the Common Room supported local volunteer 'members' to host enterprising community projects, such as Trade School Norwich, an open learning space that runs on barter (Figure 24), Common Soup, which combines communal meals with crowdfunding for good causes, and crafting workshops. All sessions were delivered by volunteers.

Figure 23 (left)
St Laurence, Norwich
– a site with much potential

Figure 24 (below)
The Common Room hosts Trade School

Figure 25 Nosferatu night at St Laurence

The Common Room project has continued, on a less frequent basis, beyond the end of the EU funding, and has spread to other venues throughout the city. It has also raised the profile of St Laurence, leading to more commercial hire such as for themed cinema evenings (Figure 25). We are continuing to evaluate the outcomes of the project, and hope to develop a long-term and sustainable plan for the church in the future.

Inspiring the future: our heritage learning programme

We carefully design our regeneration projects to complement the building's architecture and history, but many of our sites are simply too sensitive for any significant intervention. We have therefore developed other means to bring people into these buildings, in

Figure 26 Heritage conservation workshop

particular through our heritage learning programme, where local schools visit our churches to discover more about their history and to take part in interactive workshops.

We consider each church's specific features and links to town history to develop bespoke programmes: for example, workshops in King's Lynn focus on the town's history as a Hanseatic League trading hub.

In Norwich we have found that St John Maddermarket lends itself to heritage conservation workshops. This treasure-trove church (Figure 27) has an outstanding collection of intricately sculpted memorials, medieval brass work and image-rich stained glass.

Figure 27 (above) St John Maddermarket, Norwich – packed with imagery and art

Figure 28 (left) Ready for heritage learning activities at St John Maddermarket

Activities here have included workshops on stained glass, tile or wall-painting conservation, where schoolchildren discover how to carefully clean historic objects (replicas of course!) and repair and retouch where necessary (Figure 26), workshops on how to 'read' a church (architectural features, materials, monuments), as well as sessions focusing on the church's strong links to lord mayors of Bristol. We have built a highly successful partnership with the Norwich Free School, and 723 schoolchildren have taken part in activities linked to St John Maddermarket (Figure 28). We are always on the lookout for new partnerships at all our churches.

New uses by night: Champing™

Champing™ – church camping – is our latest initiative to get a wider audience appreciating our churches. Inspired by 'glamping', the concept is simple: we provide camper beds, electric candles and basic loos; you bring bedding, a torch, and respect for the surroundings but also a sense of fun. We have arrangements with local farmers and pubs to provide breakfast, and champers are guaranteed an undisturbed night with the church to themselves (Figure 29).

Champing™ has really captured people's attention since it launched last year. We've had coverage in the *Telegraph*, the *Daily Mail*, the *Guardian* and in newspapers across the Netherlands, Germany, America and even Australia. This has brought unprecedented attention to the activities of the CCT, and has attracted a more diverse demographic to our sites, particularly younger urbanites (Figure 30). We hope this will encourage a whole new generation to become interested in England's historic churches – and have already seen encouraging cases of Champers becoming CCT supporters, members and volunteers.

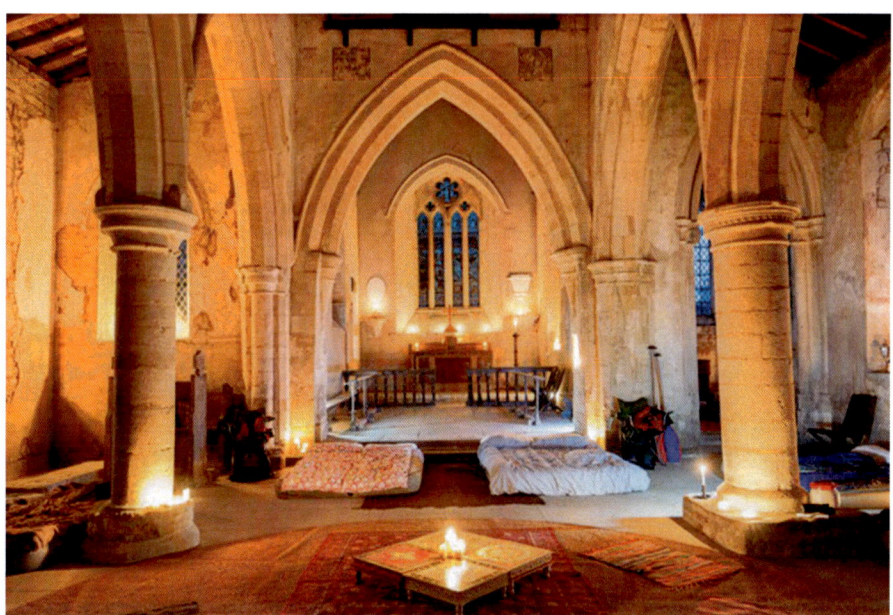

Figure 29 All set for Champing™ in All Saints, Aldwincle, Northants

Figure 30 (top) Champing™ in St John, Duxford

Figure 31 (centre) St Michael, Booton – exterior

Figure 32 (left) One of Whitwell Elwin's local angels

Figure 33
Sleeping under the angels
at Booton

From four pilot sites, ten churches are open for Champing™ this year, including Norfolk's extraordinary St Michael the Archangel church in Booton, known as the Cathedral of the Fields (Figure 31). This church was the brainchild of the eccentric clergyman Whitwell Elwin, who rebuilt the church in the late 19th century after his own design, taking elements from his favourite church buildings across England (the west doors from Glastonbury Abbey, stained glass windows from Temple Balsall, Warwickshire, a typically East Anglian angel roof), from his own imagination (the twin towers set 45 degrees from the church plan, the minaret-like central pinnacle), and even from his personal acquaintance (the angels bear likenesses to local women who contributed to the project, Figure 32). The result is a remarkably eccentric construction that would be as at home in Disneyland as in the Norfolk countryside. With its easy access to the Bure Valley Railway and to the Norfolk coast, Booton is proving one of our more popular Champing™ churches, and this unique church is finally getting the appreciation it deserves (Figure 33).

We hope to expand Champing™ to further CCT sites in future years, including in the north and west of England, but are also hoping to form partnerships with other church organizations to spread the concept further. We have already had interesting in franchising the concept from churches as far away as Orkney.

Our religious heritage – past, present and future

This is a still challenging time but one with many new opportunities. Once-secure funding streams are drying up, and there is little prospect of them ever coming back. For religious heritage organizations this is particularly problematic, as the move to a secular society has meant younger generations simply do not have the same connection to church buildings as their parents and grandparents. There is a real danger that our rich religious heritage, and with it the histories of local communities nationwide, will be completely forgotten about, and lost forever.

Yet churches have adapted to changing times throughout history. Pre-Reformation they were the first community centres, meeting places and marketplaces. They successfully adapted first to Puritan stern, silent places exclusively for worship, then to the more relaxed religious culture of Anglicanism. They can adapt to a changing society today.

We need to make an effort. We need to find uses for buildings that are driven by local communities' needs and demands, and involve people in the process every step of the way. We need to make churches attractive to new audiences and demographics. We need to reach out to young people who, as the product of several generations of non-attendance, otherwise have no link to church buildings.

This isn't easy, but there are exciting possibilities. Churches were the first community centres; they can become centres of community again. And in doing so, we can preserve our remarkable heritage and history for future generations.

Peter Aiers has worked at the Churches Conservation Trust since 2007, following a background in conservation and regeneration at English Heritage, local authorities and the Church of England. He set up the CCT's Regeneration Taskforce, and oversaw the early stages of the Bolton, King's Lynn and Ipswich projects. He is now the Director for the North and South East regions.

Matthew McKeague is the Director of Regeneration at the Churches Conservation Trust. He joined the CCT in 2008 following a background in regeneration and project management in several local authorities and in a public policy and regeneration consultancy, including as project manager for Lambeth Savings and Credit Union during the lead up to its launch.

Edward Walkington is on secondment to the Churches Conservation Trust's Regeneration Taskforce from the civil service, most recently working on mental health policy. He has supported the successful delivery of multimillion-pound welfare-to-work programmes, and led international negotiations on lorry security. Earlier he worked in the UK and European Parliaments and for a leading public policy think tank,.

Index

Note: illustrations are indexed in **bold**. References to notes are in the form 113n2, for note 2 on page 113. Individual churches are indexed under the name of the town or city.

A

Aberdeen, Triple Kirks pub, **34**
access, public, to redundant churches, 53, 73, 97
adaptation of churches, 53
agents, property, 88–9
alcohol, consumption in redundant churches, 22, 31, 34, 36, 75
   see also cafés and bars
Aldwincle, All Saints church, **115**
Algarkirk, SS Peter and Paul, 46
Ancient Monuments Consolidation and Amendment Act (1913), 10
Andrew, Donna, 6
antiques centres, 11, 53, 74, 87
art, church *see under* church, monuments, stained glass
art galleries, 74
artists, commissions from, 80
artists' studios, 28, 56, 59, 62, 64, 74, 93–4, 96
arts organizations, 28, 29, 33, 53, 56, 59, 73–4
   see also cinema, music, theatre

B

baptism, numbers of, 11
Bed City, 36
bells, 65
Benington
   All Saints, 41–7, **43**, **45**
   Community Heritage Trust, 43–4
Beonna, the, 43–4, 47
bequests for church maintenance, 3
Betjeman, Sir John, 12, 61–2
Beveridge, William, 12
birds, in churches, 94
Birkenhead, 29
Bishop, Canon, 64
Black Death, 48
Blackburn, 29
Blair, Tony, administration of, 14
Blomefield, Francis, 8, 73
Blomfield, Charles James, bishop of London, 20

Bodkin, Colin, 87
Bolton, All Souls church, **104–6**
Bolton Percy, 82, **83**
bookselling, in churches, 28, 53, 58, 75–6, 93, 96
Booton, St Michael the Archangel, 115, **116**, **117**
Boston, St Botolph's church, 46
Bournemouth, Tesco, 36
Boy Scouts, 25, 49
Bradwell, St Peter on the Wall, 19, **21**
Bridges, Lord/Bridges Commission, 10, 26–7
Bristol, 29
   St Paul's church, 29, 101, **102**, **103**, 104
   St Thomas's church, 97, **98**
Britain in Bloom, 80
Brooke, Lord Henry of Cumnor/Brooke Commission, 11–12, 27–8, 50–1, 65
Brown, Aaron, 66, **81**
Bulwer, Edward, 62
Burton, Jack, 73

C

cafés, bars and restaurants, in former churches, 30–1, **35**, **36**, 56–9, 75–6, 87
Call to Prayer, 73, 74
Camdenians, 7
Capper, Steve, 94
Carr, Chris, 82–3
Carttiss, Michael, 64
Cecil, Lord Robert, 4
champing, 115–17
charities, 33, 76–7, 105
   funding provided by, 85
   taking over redundant churches, 12, 52
      (*see also* Churches Conservation Trust, Norwich Historic Churches Trust)
Chartres, Richard, bishop of London, 35
Chipping Ongar, 19
Christ Apostolic Church, 35
Church Building, 29
church(es)
   artworks and monuments, 68–73
   buildings, historic non-religious uses, 64–5, 101
   buildings, pattern of religious uses, 64–5
   building, payment for, 4–5
   facilities, 55, 67, 69, 74, 88–92

church(es) cont'd
  furnishings and features, 6, 24, 65, 67, 73, 107
  private ownership, 28, 48
  rate, 3–4
  see also individual churches under names of places
Church Census (1851), 4–5
Church of England
  Advisory Board for Redundant Churches, 52
  Archbishops' Commission *see* Bridges Commission
  Church Assembly, 26
  closure policy, 20, 24–7, 35–6, 50–1, 62
  consulted by NHCT, 77
  powers over divested churches, 67
  sales of churches for commercial redevelopment, 48
  working with redundant churches, 45–6
Church of England Assembly (Powers) Act (1919), 10, 24
Churches Conservation Trust, 39n1, 97–118
  churches administered by, 12, 28–9, 33–5, 38, 97–118
  funding of, 97, 101, 104, 118
  heritage learning programme, 113–15
  as project manager/partner, 43–4
  see also Redundant Churches Fund
Churches: A Question of Conversion, 34
churchyards, 60n12, 66–7, 80–85
cinema, in redundant churches, 25, **113**
Circomedia, 101–4
circuses, 29, 101–4
'City Churches, The', 25
Civic Systems Lab, 111
Civic Voice, 106
clergy, interest in history and architecture, 8
climbing centre, 30, **31**
Closed Churchyards legislation, 66
commercial uses for churches, 27–8, 31, 48, 51, 53, 56–9, 61–2, 73–6, 86–96
community uses for churches, 25, 28–9, 36, 43–4, 48, 76, 101, 104–6, 111–13
Compulsory Church Rate Abolition Bill (1867), 4
concerts *see* music
Conservative Party, 31–2
construction of churches, funding for, 5
consultation processes, 106
Cormack, Patrick MP, 13
Council for the Protection of Rural England (CPRE), 12

Crowder, Sir John, 25

D
DanceEast, 105
Daunton, Martin, 3
death watch beetles, 93
deconsecration of churches, 52, 67
  of churchyards, 67
demolition of churches, 9–10, 19, 22–4, 29, 32, 38, 39n1, 48–9, 51, 61
Department for Culture, Media and Sport, 97
Department of the Environment, 38
Devonport, St Aubyn's church, 36
Deya, Gilbert/Deya Ministries, 32
Didmarton, St Lawrence's church, 35
Duxford, St John's church, **116**

E
East Shefford, St Thomas's church, 97, **99**
Eaton, Thomas, 52, 63
Ede, Tony, 73
Edinburgh, 1
Ellens, J. P. 4
Ellison, Gerald, bishop of Chester, 10
Elwin, Whitwell, 111–13
Enabling Act *see* Church of England Assembly (Powers) Act (1919)
English Heritage, 12, 13, 35, 55, 63, 65, 68, 106
  Inspired! campaign, 14
  see also Historic England
Evangelism/Evangelicals, 6

F
Finch, Jonathan, 2
Finlayson, Geoffrey, 5–6, 14
Fleming, Launcelot, bishop of Norwich, 11, 27, 50
Foyster, Steve, 76
Frampton, St Mary the Virgin, 46
Freiston, St James's church, **46**
Friends of Norwich (Historic) Churches, 12, 51, 63
Friends of the Norwich Historic Churches Trust, 54, 74, 77, 78
Friends of Norwich Museums, 27
Friends of St Nicholas Chapel, 107
Frostick, Raymond, 52, 63
funding for maintaining redundant churches, 13, 55, 67–8
  see also English Heritage Heritage Lottery Fund; *under* Churches Conservation Trust, Norwich Historic Churches Trust

fundraising
  advice on, 13
  by the CCT, 97
  forms of, 14
  in Norwich, 12–13, 51, 55, 67
furnishings *see* church furnishings

G

garden, medieval, 82
Georgian Group, 12, 27
Gladstone, W. E., 4
graves in redundant churches, 22–3
Greek Orthodox, 22
Groves, Nicholas, 19, 78
Guyhirn Chapel, 97, **100**

H

Hardington Bampfyle, St Mary's church, 97, **99**
Hare, W. Rowan, 12, 63
Harris, Jose, 4
Harrod, Dominick, 13
Harrod, Lady Wilhelmina (Billa), 12–13, 51
Henry VIII, king, 61
heating (and its lack) in churches, 74, 92–3, 108–9
Heavenly Gardens, 66, 80–5
Herbert, Percy, bishop of Norwich, 10, 25–6, 27
heritage trails, 15
heritage wall, **106**
Heritage Lincolnshire, 43
Heritage Lottery Fund, 8, 12, 13, 14, 15, 41, 44, 46, 55, 68, 101
Historic Churches Preservation Trust, 10, 25
see also Churches Conservation Trust
Historic England, 13, 14 , 68, 79
  see also English Heritage
Holland Coastal Group, 41–7
  Holland Coastal Co-operative, 42–3
Hollis, Patricia (later Lady Hollis), 63
Holmes, Frances and Michael, 78
House of Commons Culture, Media and Sport Committee, 1
housing, redundant churches used for, 29, **30**, 62
Howley, William, archbishop of Canterbury, 20

I

insurance of buildings, 55, 88, 95–6
Ipswich, 29
  Historic Churches Trust, 29, 52
  St Mary at the Quay/Quay Place, **109**, **110**, 111
Ipswich Journal, 4
Ishmael, George, 66

J

Jarrold, John, 12, 51
Jewson, Richard, 67
Jones, James, bishop of Liverpool, 35

K

King's Lynn
  heritage of, 113
  St Nicholas's Chapel, **107**, **108**, 109

L

Lake, Norman, 62
Lambert Jones, Richard, 20
lead roofing, 2
legislation, key, 39
  see also individual Acts by name
Leicester, Bed City, 36
Lincoln, 19, 48, 60
  Diocese of, 41–7
Liverpool
  Alma de Cuba, **36**
  Christ Church Kensington, 32
  Diocese of, 29–34
  St Cuthbert Everton, 31–2
  St James Toxteth, 32–3, **34**, 35
  St Nathaniel Edge Hill, 32
  St Peter's RC church, 36
  St Polycarp Everton, 32
  St Saviour Everton, 31
Liverpool and Wigan Churches Act (1904), 23
London
  Brick Lane Music Theatre, 36
  churches *see entry below*
  City churches, 20, 24–5, 48, 60n2
  County Council, 24
  Foundling Hospital, 3
  Friends of the City Churches, 35
  Museum of Garden History, 85
  Wren churches, 9
London churches:
  Christ Church Cosway Street, 35
  Christ Church Greyfriars, 25
  Holy Trinity Kingsway, 36
  Holy Trinity Minories, **22**, 23
  St Alban Wood Street, 40n23
  St Andrew by the Wardrobe, 40n23
  St Augustine Watling Street, 25

London churches (cont'd)
  St Christopher le Stocks, 20
  St Columbia Kingsland Road, 35
  St Dunstan in the East, 25
  St John Smith Square, 25, **26**
  St Luke Oseney Crescent, 35
  St Mark Silvertown, 36
  St Mark North Audley Street, 35
  St Mary Aldermanbury, 40n23
  St Matthew Spring Gardens, 23, **24**, 39n20
  St Michael Crooked Lane, 20, **22**
  St Mildred Bread Street, 40n23
  St Paul's Cathedral, 25
  St Stephen Coleman Street, 25
  St Swithun London Stone, 40n23
  St Thomas Bermondsey, 23
  Southwark Diocese, 23
London's Churches are Falling Down, 35
London's Churches are Fighting Back, 35

M
Madgin, Rebecca, 1
maintenance and repair (for churches), 2
  'caretaker scheme' for, 51
  funding for, 2–3,5, 8 (*see also* Heritage Lottery Fund)
  maintenance co-operatives, 41–7
  in Ipswich, 109–11
  in Norwich *see* churches by name
  by parishioners, 2
  preventive maintenance, 42
  repairs backlogs, 10
  state funding, 13
  training courses, 41
  by voluntary groups, 12, 41–7
Manchester Churches Act (1906), 23
Manpower Services Commission, 14
martial arts, 28, 37, 74
masons, guild of, 56, 73
media coverage, 30, 61–2
Merriman, Lord, 25
Mission and Pastoral Measure 2011, 36, 39n1
monuments
  in Norwich churches, 69–70, **71**, 74, 89–90
Morning Post, 1
Morris, Richard, 6–7
Morris, William, 9
museums, churches used as, 27, 29, **49**, 61, 63–4
music
  festival in Norwich, 1
  teaching in former church, 73, 77

venues in former churches, 25–6, 61, 74, 103

N
Nicholson, Godfrey MP, 25
non-conformists, 4
  use of Anglican churches by, 21, 32, 56
Norfolk Archaeological Trust, 27
Norfolk Association of Architects, 12
Norfolk Churches Trust, 14, 51
Norfolk Country Churches and the Future, 13
Norfolk County Council, 63–4
Norfolk Museums Service, 63
Norfolk and Norwich Archaeological Association, 8, 15
Norfolk Society, 13
Norfolk Wildlife Trust, 66, 82
Norwich
  1945 plan, 1
  1967 *Draft Urban Plan*, 1
  Austin Friars, 19, 48
  Blackfriars, 48, 61
  Bridewell Museum, 63
  Carnary College, 61
  Chapelfield Plain, 80
  churches *see entry below*
  Common room, the, 111–13
  Coslany parish, 11
  demography vs pattern of churches, 11, 49, 61
  Domesday coverage, 2
  Free School, 111
  Great Hospital, 61
  Head in the Clouds, 64
  housing, 61
  King Edward VI School, 61
  Mousehold Heath Conservators, 12
  music festival, 1
  number of churches, 48, 49
  press coverage of, 1
  St Andrew's Hall, 1
  Strangers, 48
  Strangers Hall, 63, 65
  Swan Yard, 82, 84
  walks, guided, 82, **83**
Norwich Arts Centre, 28, 73–4
Norwich churches, 28–9, 48–96
  All Saints, 56, **57**, 65
  artworks and monuments, 68–73
  'caretaker scheme' for, 51
  Cathedral, 2–3, 50, 60n6, 65
  Christ Church New Catton, 5, 13

churchyards, 60n12, 66–7, 80–5
history book, 78
Holy Trinity, 48
Old Meeting House, 77–8
proposed for redundancy, 11–12, 19, 48–52, 62
research into, 78
Roman Catholic chapel, Fishergate, 77
St Andrew, 51, 63
St Augustine, 12, 51, 97, **100**
St Benedict, 4, 49
St Christopher, 48
St Clement (at Fyebridge), 4, 50, 55, 56, 73
St Edmund Fishergate, 4, 49, 56, 73, **75**
St Ethelbert, 48
St Etheldreda, 48, 49, 50, **52**, 56, **66**, 74
St George Colegate, **3**, 4, 13, 14–15, 50, 51, 73
St George Tombland, 13, 48, 51
St Giles on the Hill, 50, 60n3
St Gregory (Pottergate), 4, **11**, 12, **53**, 55, 56, 63–4, 65, 68, **69**, **70**, **71**, 74
St Helen, 51
St James Pockthorpe, 4, 5, 14, 49, 56, 73
St John Colegate, 48
St John Evangelist, 48
St John Maddermarket, 4, 12, 51, 63, 93, **114**
St John de Sepulchre, 4, 14, 50, 51, 55, 56, 65, 68, 73, **76**
St John Timberhill, 51
St Julian, 28, 49, 50, 51, 62
St Laurence/Lawrence, 4, 12, 50, 60n3, 62, 97, 111, **112**, **113**
St Margaret Newbridge, 48
St Margaret de Westwick, 4, 55, 56, 60n4, 66, 74, 82, **84**
St Mark, Lakenham, 4, 5, 13, 50
St Martin at Oak, 4, 49, **54**, 59, 73, **77**
St Martin at Palace, 5, **7**, 14, 49, 59, 74, 77
St Mary Coslany, 4, 50, 51, 59, 62, **66**, **81**, 86–96, **87**, **89**, **90**, **91**, **93**, **94**
St Mary the Less, 48, 61, 78
St Mary in the Marsh, 51, 60n6
St Matthew at Palace, 48, 49
St Michael Conesford, 19, **21**, 48
St Michael (Miles) Coslany, 14, 59, 65, 66, 68–9, 74, 90
St Michael at Plea, 12, 50, **57**, **58**, 59, 67, 74, 75–6
St Michael at Thorn, 4, 49
St Michael Tombland, 48

St Paul, 4, 49
St Peter Hungate, **9**, 27, **28**, 40n30, 48–9, 59, 61, **62**, 67, **72**
St Peter Mancroft, 2–3, 50
St Peter Parmentergate, **37**, 50, 51, 53–4, 59, 69, 71, 73, 74
St Peter Southgate, 48, 61
St Philip Heigham, 62
St Saviour, 49, **50**, 59, 73
SS Simon and Jude, 27, 48, **49**, 59, 61, 67, 75
St Stephen, 51, 65, 80, **81**, 83, **84**
St Swithin, 4, 49, **55**, 59, 65, 73–4
Norwich City Council/Corporation, 12, 49, 51–3, 54, 55, 60, 61–3, 66–8, 78, 82, 86
councillors, 61, 63, 65, 86
Norwich Community Church, 73
Norwich Diocesan Society for Building and Enlarging Churches, 5, 6, 14
Norwich Historic Churches Trust, 50–96
conferences, 78
conservation of artworks and monuments, 68–73
conservation management plan, 68, 79
constitution and purpose, 52–6, 63, 79
facilities in churches, 67
founding of, 12, 27, 50, 52, 63
funding of, 53, 55, 63, 67–8
fundraising by, 13, 55, 67–8
grant aid to, 14
lease of churches, 52, 76–7, 87–8
office, 53–4
reassessment of operation, 55–6
repairs to churches, 52, 54–5, 63, 67–8
staff, 53
tenants, 67, 73, 74–7, 86–96
trustees, 53–4, 65, 66, 67, 76, 79, 86, 88, 96
uses of churches, 28, 56–9, 73–5, 111
website, 78
see also Friends of the Norwich Historic Churches Trust, Heavenly Gardens
Norwich Night Shelter, 28, 73
Norwich Preservation Trust, 67
Norwich Puppet Theatre, 73
Norwich Society, 12, 27, 66, 85
Norwich, bishops of, *see* Fleming, Launcelot; Herbert, Percy; Wood, Maurice
Nugent, Edward, earl of Milltown, 22

O

Observer, the, 1
Omarji, Inayat, 104–5

organs, 54
Orthodox churches, 22, 28, 29, 58, 61, 75
Oxford Movement, 8

P

Parish, Steve, 29
parishes
  secular administrative role, 4
  'super-parishes' for Norwich, 50–1, 63
Parkin, Charles, 8
Pastoral Measure (1968), 10, 26, 39n1, 51
Patterson, N. J., 32
Perry Lithgow Partnership, 69, 70
Peto, Sir Samuel Morton, 22
Phillimore Report, 23–4
Piggott, Stuart, 8
Pilgrim's Trust, 10
planning controls, 10
Pordham, Colin, 76
Preston, 29
  St Mark's church, **30**
Protecting and Preserving Our Heritage, 1–2
Protestant Reformers Memorial Church, 32
puppet theatre, 5

Q

Quinn, Rory, 63
quinquennial inspection reports, 42

R

Razey, Keith, 96
redundancy of churches
  16th century and earlier, 48
  categories for main future use, 20
  early investigation, 10
  in London, 20, 24–5, 48
  in Norwich, 11–12, 19, 48–96
  preservation (without alternative use), 19
  and return to use as church, 32–3, 35
  and subsequent use *see* uses
  see also deconsecration
Redundant Churches Fund, 10, 12, 27, 33, 51
  funding of, 12
  see also Churches Conservation Trust
Redundant Churches and Other Religious Buildings Act (1969), 10, 12, 39n1
Reorganisation of Areas Measures (1944–54), 10, 24, 26
repair *see* maintenance and repair
restoration of church features
  often not done in 19th century, 6
  see also maintenance and repair

Rochester, 19
Rodger, Richard, 1
Round Tower Society, 95
Rowe, Ken, 67
Royal Fine Art Commission, 10
ruined churches, 28

S

Sainsbury, Roger, 32
saints, Danish-heritage, 2
St Stephen the Great, 76
SAVE, 35
Saxon Shore Co-Op, 47
Scotland, former church uses in, 36
sculpture, in churchyards, 83–4
Second World War, damage to churches in, 10, 24, 40n2, 49, 62
security issues, 82, 94–5
Shepherd, David, 33
Shore, Peter MP, 13
Shrewsbury, St Mary's Church, 97, **98**
Sikh temples, 32, **33**
Simmonds, Paul, 86–7
Socialism, 39n13
Society of Antiquaries, 10
Society for the Protection of Ancient Buildings (SPAB), 9, 41–7
  Faith in Maintenance project, 41
  Maintenance Cooperatives Project, 41–2
Southampton, Singh Sabha Gurdwara, **33**
SPCK, 75–6
Spirit of Place, 9
squirrels, 90
stained glass, **72**, 89, 94, 95, 114
Stamford, 19
Suffolk Mind, 109, 111
Sweet, Rosemary, 8

T

Tanner, Norman, 3
Templeman Report, 35
tenants of churches, 75–7, 86–96
  methods of identifying, 86–7
  negotiations with, 76, 88
  responsible for fitments, 53
Tesco, 36
theatre
  medieval, in churches, 101
  in redundant churches, 32, 36, 73
Thetford, 48, 60
Thurnam, W. Digby, 23
Tilsley, Gordon, 52, 56, 60, 63, 67

Town Close Trust, 85
Town and Country Planning Acts (1944, 1947), 10
Town and Country Planning Act (1968), 10
Townroe, Peter, 1

U

Union of Benefices Act (1860), 9, 20, 22, 26
Union of Benefices Act and measures (1920s), 10, 22, 24, 26
Union of Benefices Measure (1952), 25, 26
Union of Continguous Benefices Act (1545), 19
University of East Anglia, 107
uses for redundant churches, 19–40
 in CCT churches, 97–113
 controversial proposed uses, 22–3, 25, 27, 30–1, 36, 75, 86
 early uses, 19, 23, 27, 48, 61
 in Norwich, 12, 28, 53, 56–9, 69–75
 by non-Christian religious groups, 32, **33**, 77
 by other Christian denominations, 21–2, 27–9, 32, 33, 58, 75–6
 statistics on, 38
 see also commercial uses, community uses, *under* other specific uses
uses, early of extant churches, 64–5

V

vandalism, 95–6
Victoria & Albert Museum, 34, 70
Victorian society, 30
visitors to redundant churches, 89, 95

volunteers/voluntary sector, 1–3
 in 18th and 19th centuries, 3–4
 Beveridge's report on, 12
 for the Heavenly Gardens project, 80–5
 with the Norwich Historic Churches Trust, 53
 state involvement/control, 14
 trained in maintenance, 41–6, 114
 trained in visitor services, 47
 working with CCT, 107, 111

W

walks, guided, 82, **83**
wall paintings, 68, **69**, **70**
war *see* Second World War
Warrington
 St Ann's church, 29–30, **31**
 St Peter's church, 30–1
Warrington Guardian, 30
Webb, Jack, 33
Weinstein, Ben, 9
welfare
 moral hazard of providing, 6
 role of state in, 5–6
Westwood, Bill, 63
Wharf, the, 77
Wilberforce, Samuel, bishop of Oxford, 21
Wolfgang and Heron, 80
Wood, Maurice, bishop of Norwich, 13

Y

York, 19, 29, 52

Join the Friends
of the Norwich Historic Churches Trust

Why not join a convivial group that works to support Norwich's wonderful heritage of redundant churches? We fundraise to support the Norwich Historic Churches Trust which manages many of the churches, and organize regular events for members.
 Learn more, and download a membership form, from our website:

www.fnhct.org.uk

This is the first collaboration between the Norwich Historic Churches Trust and the Lasse Press: an eclectic and highly readable selection of illustrated essays, focused on the broad theme of medieval church-related history, and mostly, though not exclusively, on Norwich's extraordinary legacy of medieval churches. All profits from the sale of the book go to support the work of the Norwich Historic Churches Trust.

Contents: Foreword *Brian Ayers* ♦ Toothache, saints, and churches in medieval Norfolk, with particular reference to the City of Norwich *John Beal* ♦ Theology to liturgy: the material culture of change in Norwich and beyond, c.1450–1640 *Victor Morgan* ♦ Roman Catholic chapels of Norwich *Francis Young* ♦ The sheep hath paid for all: stained glass and self-expression in the Late Middle Ages *Allan Barton* ♦ Valuations of churches in the medieval diocese of Norwich *Elizabeth Gemmill* ♦ The funeral of John Paston *Susan Curran*

Available from bookshops and direct from the publisher via
www.lassepress.com

For details of hard copy and electronic editions of titles published by the Lasse Press, visit:

www.lassepress.com